W9-CDF-096

COMPREHENSIVE RESEARCH
AND STUDY GUIDE

BLOOM'S
MAJOR
SHORT STORY
WRITERS

Anton

Chekhov

EDITED AND WITH AN
INTRODUCTION BY HAROLD BLOOM

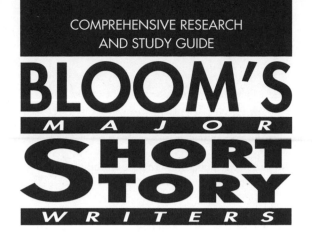

COMPREHENSIVE RESEARCH
AND STUDY GUIDE

BLOOM'S

MAJOR

SHORT STORY

WRITERS

Anton

Chekhov

EDITED AND WITH AN INTRODUCTION BY HAROLD BLOOM

© 2001 by Chelsea House Publishers, a subsidiary of
Haights Cross Communications.

Introduction © 2001 by Harold Bloom.

Printed and bound in the United States of America.

First Printing
1 3 5 7 9 8 6 4 2

Library of Congress Cataloging-in-Publication Data

Anton Chekhov / edited and with an introduction by Harold Bloom.
        p. cm. — (Bloom's major poets)
    Includes bibliographical references and index.
    ISBN 0-7910-5942-1 (alk. paper)
    1. Chekhov, Anton Pavlovich, 1860–1904—Criticism and
interpretation—Handbooks, manuals, etc. 2. Chekhov, Anton Pavlovich,
1860–1904—Examinations—Study guides. 3. Short story—Handbooks,
manuals, etc. I. Bloom, Harold. II. Series.

PG3458.Z9 F532 2000
891.72'3--dc21   00-059629
                                            CIP

Chelsea House Publishers
1974 Sproul Road, Suite 400
Broomall, PA 19008-0914

The Chelsea House World Wide Web address is
http://www.chelseahouse.com

Contributing Editor: Mirjana Kalezic

Produced by: Robert Gerson Publisher's Services, Santa Barbara, CA

11/7/02 $22.95

Contents

User's Guide

This volume is designed to present biographical, critical, and bibliographical information on the author's best-known or most important short stories. Following Harold Bloom's editor's note and introduction is a detailed biography of the author, discussing major life events and important literary accomplishments. A plot summary of each short story follows, tracing significant themes, patterns, and motifs in the work, and an annotated list of characters supplies brief information on the main characters in each story.

A selection of critical extracts, derived from previously published material from leading critics, analyzes aspects of each short story. The extracts consist of statements from the author, if available, early reviews of the work, and later evaluations up to the present. A bibliography of the author's writings (including a complete list of all books written, cowritten, edited, and translated), a list of additional books and articles on the author and the work, and an index of themes and ideas in the author's writings conclude the volume.

❧

Harold Bloom is Sterling Professor of the Humanities at Yale University and Henry W. and Albert A. Berg Professor of English at the New York University Graduate School. He is the author of over 20 books, including *Shelley's Mythmaking* (1959), *The Visionary Company* (1961), *Blake's Apocalypse* (1963), *Yeats* (1970), *A Map of Misreading* (1975), *Kabbalah and Criticism* (1975), *Agon: Toward a Theory of Revisionism* (1982), *The American Religion* (1992), *The Western Canon* (1994), and *Omens of Millennium: The Gnosis of Angels, Dreams, and Resurrection* (1996). *The Anxiety of Influence* (1973) sets forth Professor Bloom's provocative theory of the literary relationships between the great writers and their predecessors. His most recent books include *Shakespeare: The Invention of the Human*, a 1998 National Book Award finalist, and *How to Read and Why*, which was published in 2000.

Professor Bloom earned his Ph.D. from Yale University in 1955 and has served on the Yale faculty since then. He is a 1985 MacArthur Foundation Award recipient, served as the Charles Eliot Norton Professor of Poetry at Harvard University in 1987–88, and has received honorary degrees from the universities of Rome and Bologna. In 1999, Professor Bloom received the prestigious American Academy of Arts and Letters Gold Medal for Criticism.

Currently, Harold Bloom is the editor of numerous Chelsea House volumes of literary criticism, including the series BLOOM'S NOTES, BLOOM'S MAJOR DRAMATISTS, BLOOM'S MAJOR NOVELISTS, MAJOR LITERARY CHARACTERS, MODERN CRITICAL VIEWS, MODERN CRITICAL INTERPRETATIONS, and WOMEN WRITERS OF ENGLISH AND THEIR WORKS.

Editor's Note

My Introduction meditates upon "The Darling," a story that the great Tolstoy loved. As this volume contains twenty-eight critical views upon five stories, I will mention here only a few that seem to me particularly useful.

On "The Kiss," the critic V. S. Pritchett emphasizes Chekhov's qualification of the military mystique, while Ronald L. Johnson catches the almost unbearable poignance of "Rothschild's Fiddle."

The life-affirming force of "The Student" is celebrated by Robert L. Jackson, after which Donald Rayfield reads "The Darling" as a presentation of Chekhov's passion for life.

There are ten critical extracts concerning "The Lady with the Dog." Perceptive as all of these are, pride of place should be given to the novelist Vladimir Nabokov, who gives a broad overview of Chekhov's art as a storyteller.

Introduction

HAROLD BLOOM

Nearly a century after his death, Chekhov remains the most influential of all short story writers. There is an alternative tradition to the Chekhovian story, a rival mode invented by Kafka and developed by Borges. But such varied storytellers as James Joyce and D. H. Lawrence, Ernest Hemingway and Flannery O'Connor, essentially are part of the Chekhovian tradition (though Joyce denied it).

This brief volume examines five of Chekhov's best tales, yet I will confine this Introduction to "The Darling," Tolstoy's particular favorite. Critics have found in "The Darling" versions of the ancient Greek myths of Psyche and of Echo, and these allusions are present, but the heart of Chekhov's wonderful story is elsewhere. Tolstoy located it best when he said that the Darling, Olenka, has a soul that is "wonderful and holy." Olenka comes alive only when she lives for another, with a love so perfect that the other's concerns absorb her completely.

Though you can regard Olenka as childlike or motherly, it seems best to follow Tolstoy, who found in her a holy soul.

Maxim Gorky memorably remarked of Chekhov that in his presence "everyone felt an unconscious desire to be simpler, more truthful, more himself," an effect that can be experienced also by Chekhov's readers. Not that the skeptical, all-knowing Chekhov is another "holy soul" in Tolstoy's sense (though Tolstoy thought so, up to a point,) but undoubtedly Chekhov, like his master Shakespeare, persuades you that you can see with him what otherwise would never be apparent to you. What then can we see in "The Darling?" How should we read it, and why?

Can anyone, in reality, be so whole-hearted as Olenka? And yet, "whole-hearted" is misleading, if only because poor Olenka is reduced to an absolute emptiness when she does not have someone to love. So extreme does her condition become that it requires all of Chekhov's tact to teach us, implicitly but firmly, to avoid the vulgarity of conjectures as to her pathology. She has no opinions of her own, and yet is "a gentle, soft-hearted, compassionate girl," who lacks only a sense of self, which she can acquire only in loving. To see her as the female victim of a patriarchal society would be absurd: how would you go about raising her consciousness? There always have been and will be some like her, perhaps many, and men as well as women. Tolstoy's religious ideas were very much his own, and yet one can understand the particular sense in which this Darling or "little soul" is holy. John Keats said that he believed in nothing but the holiness of the heart's affections, and William Blake proclaimed that everything that lives is holy. Olenka is holy in that way. Keats added that he believed also in the truth of the imagination, but Olenka cannot imagine without being guided by the heart's affections.

Chekhov, like Shakespeare, solves no problems, makes no decisions for us, and quests for the total truth of the human, in the precise sense of Shakespeare's invention of the human. Olenka, though doubtless very Russian, is also universal. Chekhov's stance towards her is ironical only in a Shakespearean way: the wheel comes full circle, and we are here. Life, which has taken three men away from Olenka, restitutes her with a foster-son, for whom she can survive. Shakespeare, as a stage dramatist, could not afford to represent banality, since even he could not hold an audience with our ordinary unhappiness. Chekhov, Shakespearean to his core, employed his stories to do what even his own plays could not do: illuminate the commonplace, without exalting or distorting it. *Three Sisters*, Chekhov's most remarkable drama, could not afford a character like Olenka, even in a minor part. It is a kind of literary miracle that Chekhov could center "The Darling" so fully upon Olenka, who can come alive only through a complete love for someone else. ❀

Biography of
Anton Chekhov

Leo Tolstoy, Chekhov's greatest contemporary, called Chekhov "Pushkin in prose" comparing him with Russia's greatest poet. Today, when Chekhov holds a place among the greatest Russian writers, this compliment seems natural. But at the end of the 19th century—the century of the great novels of Balzac, Stendhal, Tolstoy, Dostoevsky, and Dickens—Tolstoy's compliment confirmed Chekhov's mastery of a then-small literary genre—the short story.

Anton Pavlovich Chekhov's grandfather had been a serf who succeeded in acquiring the considerable wealth of 3,500 rubles in order to purchase freedom for himself and his family. Anton was born on January 17, 1860, the third of six children, at Taganrog, a Russian port on the sea of Azov. Chekhov had ambivalent feelings about the provincial town in which he spent his first nineteen years. Reminiscing later in life, he remembered it as "utterly Asiatic: such oriental squalor on all sides that I can't believe my eyes. Sixty thousand inhabitants do nothing but eat, drink, reproduce themselves. Of other interests they have none." In the late 1890s, he was to become Taganrog's cultural benefactor, presenting hundreds of books to its library and patronizing the local museum. He also used it as a background in his stories "Lights" (1888), "Doctor Startsev" (1898), and "A Hard Case" (1898).

At the age of 7, he was enrolled at the school for Greek boys (since Greeks dominated commerce in Taganrog) where he wasted a year before he became a student in Taganrog classical *gimnazya* (grammar school). Harsh discipline was imposed in the grammar schools, and they resembled military establishments rather than educational institutions. When Chekhov was 16, his father's business rapidly deteriorated, and the family had to flee to Moscow in order to avoid their creditors. Anton was left alone in Taganrog to finish the school. For next three years, he supported himself by coaching younger boys and was even able to send some money to his family in Moscow. Chekhov would, during all his life, help not only his father and mother, but his brothers and a sister: his feeling for family was very strong and he once remarked, without ill will, that the family was his "benign tumor."

During these years he showed a natural inclination towards mimicry, play-acting, and practical jokes. When a public library opened in 1876, a whole new world became accessible to him. He read the works of novelist Victor Hugo, naturalist/explorer Alexander von Humboldt, and philosopher Arthur Schopenhauer, as well as books by such Russian radicals as Belinsky, Dobrolyobov, Pisarev, and Herzen. Still, none of Chekhov's early activities promised a remarkable literary career.

In 1879, after having finished school, he joined his family in Moscow and began to study medicine at the University of Moscow. But he couldn't give up writing. For the first years of his literary career, he wrote mostly for newspapers and journals. His output in those years was incredible: he wrote approximately two stories per week for the next four years. Although these stories generally are not as good as Chekhov's later work, he did create a few masterpieces during that time of mass production: "Joke" and "Sorrow" among them. His stories appeared under his pen name Antosha Chekhonte; this period of his work is usually referred to as the Antosha Chekhonte Period.

Anton was 24 when he completed studies of medicine and got a job in the hospital in Vaskrensensk. His first book of collected stories, *Skazki Melpomeny* (*Tales of Melpomene*) came out in 1884. His second collection, *Pyotrye rasskazy* (*Motley Tales*, 1886) was an immediate success with the public. This book also attracted the attention of two influential men. One was Dmitry Grigorovich, a Russian novelist and short-story writer. In a letter to Chekhov, Grigorovich wrote that the younger man had "real talent . . . which sets you far above other writers of the younger generation." Grigorovich also introduced Chekhov to Aleksey Suvorin, the publisher of *Novoye vremya* (New Times). Suvorin hired Chekhov as a regular contributor to his publication and became his close friend. With this more financially secure position, Chekhov could write fewer stories and concentrate on improving their quality. At about this time, Chekhov also wrote his first play, *Ivanov*, which was produced in Moscow in 1887. His short story "The Kiss" was written the same year. In 1888 his long story "The Steppe" won the prestigious Pushkin Award.

Chekhov had suffered from tuberculosis from an early age but at the age of twenty-four he experienced his first serious hemorrhage.

As a doctor, he saw many friends and relatives who had suffered and died from tuberculosis. After his brother's death in 1889 he used his writing to surmount the depression caused by knowing he would not live long.

In 1890, despite his illness, he visited the prison island, Sakhalin, in the Far East. Sakhalin had been a convicts' settlement for three decades. Chekhov published his observations and experiences in *Ostrov Sakhalin* (*Sakhalin Island*, 1891).

After his return home, Chekhov became involved in famine relief work. He also bought a piece of land at Melikhovo, fifty miles south of Moscow. In 1894 he wrote several important stories at Melikhovo, including the long stories "Ward No. 6" and "My Life," and the short stories "The Student" and "Rothschild's Fiddle." During this period Chekhov also wrote his first major plays, *Uncle Vanya* (1890) and *The Seagull* (1896). Unfortunately, the first performance of *The Seagull*, at the State Theater of St. Petersburg, was such a complete failure that Chekhov vowed to give up playwriting. He persevered, however, and in 1898 *The Seagull* was put on by the newly formed Moscow Theatre and became a great success.

Chekhov remained at Melikhovo (his parents, sister, and younger brother settled with him) until 1898, when the state of his health forced him to move to Yalta, a Crimean health resort. While in Yalta, he often met with fellow writers Leo Tolstoy and Maxim Gorky. (Gorky magnificently caught the characters of both writers in his 1919 book *Reminiscences of Tolstoy, Chekhov and Andreyev*.) Chekhov also married a well-known actress, Olga Knipper, in 1901. During this time, Chekhov's attention was mostly turned to writing plays, although he did produce some very good stories, "The Lady with the Dog" and "The Darling" (1899), the long story "In the Ravine" (1900), "The Bishop" (1902), and "Betrothed" (1903), among them. His play *The Three Sisters* was produced in 1901, and *The Cherry Orchard* was produced on January 17, 1904, in honor of his 44th birthday. In June of the same year his illness had advanced so much that he had to go to a small health resort in Badenweiler, Germany. Anton Chekhov died there on July 2, 1904. ✿

Plot Summary of
"The Kiss"

Chekhov is reported to have written "The Kiss" in two days during December 1887. The first paragraph is an example of almost military punctuality quite appropriate for a story with military background. "At eight o'clock on the evening of the twentieth of May all the six batteries" are quartered in the village of Myestetchki. When they are invited by a messenger to a reception given by a retired officer, Lieutenant-General von Rubbek, the officers accept reluctantly. They are tired, longing for bed, and they still remember vividly a party the previous year when a retired army officer gave them food and drink but became so carried away by their presence that he told anecdotes of his glorious past the whole night, refusing to let them go to their quarters.

The general, on the other hand, would rather not host the officers, as his house is full of relatives. He invites them because he feels it is his social obligation to do so.

Chekhov suggests the atmosphere of the house by describing small details of setting and background: the sounds of waltz music, the spring fragrance of roses and lilac trees. Although the officers feel awkward, most are able to enjoy the party because there are women present. One who does not is the story's protagonist, Ryabovitch, "the shyest, most modest and most undistinguished officer in the whole brigade." Wishing to take at least some part in the evening, he follows some officers, who have been invited to play billiards, into another room. The players take no notice of him and he grows weary and feels that he is not wanted. On his way back to the main room, however, he pauses hesitantly in one dark room. Suddenly, a woman enters; she embraces and kisses him, mistakenly believing that Ryabovitch is her lover. Realizing the error, she cries out and flees the room.

This trivial adventure has an astonishing effect upon Ryabovitch. The reader enters thus into what critics have termed the Chekhovian state of mind (*Chékhoskoye nastroyénie*): that is, that life's transience acts fatally upon human beings and modifies forever their assumptions about themselves. Chekhov illuminates the terrain of Ryabovitch's soul: "He gave himself entirely to the new sensation which he had never experienced before in his life— Something strange was happening to him. . . . His neck ⟨. . .⟩ seem⟨s⟩ to be anointed with oil; on his left cheek," where he was mistakenly kissed, he feels a "chilly, tingling sensation as from peppermint drops . . ."

Ryabovitch experiences a sudden explosion of joy; he feels like dancing, talking, laughing. He forgets all about his "undistinguished appearance." Returning to the party, he tries to figure out who the unknown woman may be, and to understand what has happened. He is sensible enough to guess that apparently a girl had arranged a secret meeting with her lover in the dark room and that she mistook Ryabovitch for him. As he returns to camp, he sees a river with brilliant stars reflected in it.

The next morning, the brigade has to leave the village. When Ryabovitch looks back for the last time at the village, the author tells us, that he feels sad, "as though he were parting with something very near and dear to him." The next two pages are an account of his brigade on the march. (Chekhov captured army life so well that when the story was published, it immediately won the admiration of Russian army officers.) While moving with the brigade, Ryabovitch gives himself up to dreams: in his imagination he talks to the girl, caresses her, leans on her shoulder. Soon he is picturing dinners with a wife and children, his promotion to general and the country estate he will buy. The idea that he can also be an ordinary person, like everyone else, delights Ryabovitch.

In the evening, the brigade reaches its resting place. While he is having dinner with two of his comrades, and after a few glasses of beer, Ryabovitch is seized by an irresistible desire to share his new sensations with his colleagues. It stuns him that it takes such a short time to tell the story, and disappoints him when the other soldiers do not give his awakening the reverence he feels it deserves, going on to compare it to their own experiences. When Ryabovitch goes to bed, he vows he will never confide in anyone again.

Three months later, on August 31, the brigade returns to Myestetchki. Ryabovitch experiences an "intense longing to see the church, the insincere family of the Von Rubbeks, the dark room." In the following sentence, the reader hears the author's subtly ironic comment; "The 'inner voice,' which so often deceives lovers, whispered to him for some reason that he would be sure to see her . . ."

The messenger of Von Rubbek, however, fails to appear with an expected invitation and a painful uneasiness takes possession of Ryabovitch. He goes by himself to the church, and when he reaches the Baron's house he finds it dark and quiet. On his way back to the river, he passes by the bath-house, where the bath towels are hanging on the rail. The touching of the cold damp bath towel has a sobering effect upon him and it triggers the powerful final moment of the story. Ryabovitch looks down to the river "How stupid, how stupid! How unintelligent it all is." Through the medium of hero's mind, we witness a drastic emotional change. It no longer seems to him strange that he wouldn't see the girl that kissed him accidentally. Rather, he feels just the opposite: it would be unusual if he saw her again. The soldier's dreams are shattered; he feels "the whole world, the whole life" has become "an unintelligible, aimless jest."

When he arrives back at the camp, the orderly reports that his comrades have all gone to "General Fontryabakin's party." By setting the general's name within quotation marks (the message is related to Ryabovitch through indirect discourse), Chekhov calls the reader's attention to a strange pronunciation of General von Rubbek's name. Does the orderly mispronounce the name or does Ryabovitch mishear it?

The story closes with Ryabovitch going to bed "in his wrath with his fate, as though to spite it, he did not go to the General's." The dream that has sustained his existence for the last three months is irretrievably gone.

"The Kiss" captures the essence of the term Chekhovian: it is not something that happens or does not happen that matters, but the way that thing felt. In Chekhov's work, extraordinary moments are rare, and they are devoured in life's daily routine. Critics are correct in calling Chekhov's stories "biographies of a mood" or "studies in atmosphere." ❁

List of Characters in
"The Kiss"

Captain Ryabovitch is an officer in an artillery brigade. He has sloping shoulders and whiskers like a lynx. He is a shy man, ill at ease in the company of other people. His monotonous existence is disturbed by an unknown woman's accidental kiss.

General von Rubbek is a retired army officer, about 60 years old, who invites the officers of the artillery brigade to a party at his home. Although insincere in his invitation, he behaves with courtesy.

Lieutenant Lobytko incessantly talks "interesting nonsense" trying desperately to seduce a young woman. The author notes that, "had he been intelligent, he might have concluded that she would never call him to heel."

Lieutenant Merzlyakov, in contrast to Lobytko, is a silent, peaceable man, who is considered to be highly educated officer. He constantly reads a periodical called "Vyestnik Evropi." ❀

Critical Views on
"The Kiss"

NATHAN ROSEN ON THE DEVASTATING RESOLUTION OF
THE STORY

[Nathan Rosen is a professor of Russian at the University of
Rochester, New York. He is also the author of the book
Fiction of Leonid Leonov (1961). In this extract, Rosen
examines the protagonist's joy and shows how Chekhov
prepares his readers for the devastating end of the story.]

He gave himself up to the new sensation which he had never
experienced before in his life. Something strange was happening to
him. . . . His neck, round which soft, fragrant arms had so lately been
clasped, seemed to him to be anointed with oil; on his left cheek near
his mustache where the unknown had kissed him there was a faint
chilly tingling sensation as from peppermint drops, and the more he
rubbed the place the more distinct was the chilly sensation; all of him,
from head to foot, was full of a strange new feeling which grew
stronger and stronger. . . . He wanted to dance, to talk, to run into the
garden, to laugh aloud. . . . He quite forgot that he was round-
shouldered and uninteresting. . . .

This sudden explosion of joy and life is followed by an imaginative
effort to find out who the unknown girl was. After mentally
dismissing each of the young ladies at the party for having one
blemish or another, he tries to create an ideal girl composed of the
most attractive features of all the girls present.

This outburst of joy and fantasizing is never explained by
Chekhov, but at least three factors are clear. In resigning himself to
the role of an onlooker Ryabovich has repressed the force of life
within him. We get glimpses of that force in his sensitive
appreciation of the von Rabbek family and his desire "to take some
part in the general movement." Moreover, his normal self-control
and resignation have weakened in the atmosphere of the party—the
perfumes, music, flowers, springtime, and brandy. Even in the dark
room where the adventure took place "the windows were wide open
and there was a smell of poplars, lilacs, and roses . . . ," while a
mazurka could be heard in the next room. The novel sensations are
continued in the description of the embrace and the kiss: soft
fragrant arms, oil, the chill of peppermint drops. Finally,

Ryabovich's monotonous life as an officer is given increasing importance as the story unfolds. The commander shouts from habit. The two officers who share Ryabovich's billet are bores: one seeks women and beer constantly (and is further debunked by not having a mustache); the other is constantly reading a periodical, *The Messenger of Europe,* as proof that he is highly educated. Therefore, a romantic milieu, new sensations, and a kiss stimulate a sleeping imagination.

If Ryabovich's adventure is a fantasy, its effect and continuing power over him have a solid foundation in reality: the adventure has awakened his dormant force of life, which from now on will express itself in joy, in the exercise of the unfettered imagination, and finally—and more importantly—in his conviction that he is at last taking part in the general movement (romance, marriage, family). These are by no means fantasies but hitherto suppressed needs of his whole being.

Ryabovich's joy at the novelty of his adventure evolves into a different kind of joy at the thought that he is an ordinary person who will have an ordinary destiny, that is, a wife and children. Both of these themes come to his mind as he returns with the other officers from von Rabbek's house:

> Probably the same idea occurred to each one of them as to Ryabovich: would there ever come a time for them when, like von Rabbek, they would have a large house, a family, a garden—when they too would be able to welcome people, even though insincerely, feed them, make them drunk and contented?

The officers take the path along the river. They see stars reflected in the dark water. The stars "quivered and were broken up—and from that alone it could be seen that the river was flowing rapidly." This is an objective description made by all the officers, and it is planted here to contrast with Ryabovich's subjective inference about the river later on.

Near them a nightingale trills loudly, "taking no notice of the crowd of officers," even when they stand around it. The force of life in the nightingale, the force that makes it want to sing, is greater than the fear it may have of the officers. Isn't the nightingale reflecting the force of life awakening in Ryabovich—a force greater than the dreary realism in which, "half-asleep," he has spent most of his life? The officers turn from the nightingale to speculating on the nature of a murky red light on the opposite bank. "Ryabovich, too, looked at the light, and he fancied that the light looked and winked at him, as though it knew about the kiss." ⟨...⟩

This analysis confirms Mathewson's speculation that "Chekhov's devastating resolution of the story destroys not only the illusion but Ryabovich's engagement with life as well. . . . In his final bitterness he may have lost the power to love at all, and with that his last attachment to life." Ryabovich is therefore in a far worse state at the end than he was at the beginning. Before the incident with the kiss he had been resigned to his fate as on onlooker upon life; he had lived, as Chekhov remarked, "half-asleep." After the kiss, his repressed life force was suddenly released as joy and imagination, and later it evolved into a certainty that he too was destined to "take part in the general movement"—that is, to be ordinary: to love, to marry, to have children, buy an impressive estate, and gain the rank of general. He embodied all this in his identification with Mestechki and the *rodnye* von Rabbeks, with whom he associated all that was most precious in his past, including his parents. When the messenger from the von Rabbeks failed to appear on August 31, he felt deceived and insulted, rejected by those dearest to him. The force of life, released so suddenly by the kiss of an unknown woman in a dark room, was now just as suddenly frozen in movement, violently forced back, and compelled to recoil upon Ryabovich himself, and in doing so it destroyed him.

—Nathan Rosen, "The Life Force in Chekhov's 'The Kiss,'" *Ulbandus Review* 2, no. 1 (Fall 1979): pp. 176–78, 184.

V. S. PRITCHETT ON CHEKHOV'S STORYTELLING METHOD

[V. S. Pritchett (1920–1997) was a British novelist, short-story writer, and critic known for his ironic style. His best known collections of short stories are *You Make Your Own Life* (1938), *Blind Love and Other Stories* (1969) and *More Collected Short Stories* (1983). His collections of critical essays include *The Myth Makers* (1979) and *A Man of Letters*

(1985). This extract is taken from his 1988 biography on Chekhov. Pritchett analyzes the differences between Chekhov and Turgenev and stresses the importance of occupation in Chekhov's protagonists.]

We have already been struck by the fact that the so-called connoisseur of moods is almost invariably concerned with the métier, the trades and professions of his characters, whether they are peasants, workmen, doctors, lawyers or landowners. What does occupation do to a man's nature? In *The Kiss*, the one long story he wrote in his 1887 summer at Babkino, there is an extraordinary example of Chekhov's power of absorbing the mystique of an occupation yet avoiding tedious documentation. At Babkino a brigade of artillery was stationed. It was not difficult to note the characteristics of officers and men, to catch their work, their duties, their talk in the mess, the difference between their preoccupations on the march, their care for their equipment; their "mystique" is another matter. Chekhov had read Tolstoy and Lermontov and already knows that an army is a migrant culture. He may have been told the incident of the story by a general he had met at the Kiselevs, but it would have lost all perspective if he had not, by a mixture of observation and meiosis, put a regiment on duty plainly before us as human beings.

The story opens lightly with a party. The retired General von Rabbek, local lord of the manor, has invited the officers to it. They are keen, of course, to meet the ladies. There are drinks and there is dancing. The soldiers throw themselves into the fun—all except Staff Captain Ryabovich. He can't dance or play billiards; he is a short ugly fellow who wears spectacles and has lynxlike whiskers and is shut up in himself. He wanders about with gloomy curiosity over the grand house, walks into a room, which is in darkness. Suddenly he has an experience that will haunt him for years. A girl rushes into the dark room, cries out "At last!," kisses him, then gives a scream and runs away. She has mistaken him for someone else. The ugly, shy little staff captain is transformed. He feels suddenly proud. He struts back to the ballroom and tries to guess, by a perfume or a voice, who the girl was. He fails to find out, and from now on we see a life of fantasy beginning.

The evening comes to an end. The soldiers leave and take a shortcut through the woods to their billets, shouting and laughing.

No doubt, says Chekhov, they were wondering whether *they* would someday have a mansion like the general's and whether they would be rich enough to have fine gardens and woods like these. But Ryabovich is lost in his obsession. The stars are out and their reflection trembles, dissolves and forms again in the stream he crosses, just as the misleading kiss reflects in his life. He hears—as so often occurs in Chekhov's landscape—"the plaintive cry of drowsy snipe" and "a nightingale in full song," and one of the vulgar soldiers says, "How about that! . . . the little rascal doesn't give a damn!" Here we notice one of the differences between Turgenev and Chekhov: in Chekhov the sights and sounds of nature are seen and heard by *people*. In Turgenev they are seen and heard by the detached author for their own beautiful sake. When distant lights shine through the trees, for example, Ryabovich thinks the lights know his secret. Back at the billet he is brought instantly down to earth. The batman is reporting to the commander: "Darling's foot was injured at yesterday's re-shoeing, sir. The vet put on clay and vinegar." ⟨. . .⟩

As an innovator in the writing of short stories, especially in his mastery of nostalgia and mood, Chekhov knew that his great predecessors were novelists who had addressed themselves to questions like the emergence of Russia from its prolonged medieval condition. The patrician Turgenev had made his stand for the liberation of the serfs and the example of Western civilization. Dostoyevsky had been sent to Siberia for his part in an alleged revolutionary conspiracy but had ended in denouncing the Western socialist idea and its materialism. Tolstoy, after his conversion, had turned to simple Bible teaching and to the doctrine of nonresistance to evil by force. There was now a new radical generation who were growing up as Russia became, to some degree, industrialized. In the older generation one was judged by one's "convictions"; in Chekhov's by one's "tendency."

—V. S. Pritchett, *Chekhov: A Spirit Set Free* (London: Hodder and Stoughton, 1988): pp. 42–44, 45–46.

JOSEPH L. CONRAD ON THE STORY'S ROMANTIC ASPECTS

[This extract is taken from Joseph L. Conrad's essay on three of Chekhov's stories ("Verochka," "The Kiss," and "The Black Monk"), in which Conrad studies certain romantic and diabolic elements.]

A second stage in Chekhov's use of the romantic heritage can be illustrated by "The Kiss," where the contrast between the real and the ideal is central. In this story there is regular interaction between the routine details of military life and the hero's fanciful imagination, which is stimulated by sensory perceptions associated with the garden. As we will see, the garden itself is brought inside, both inside the drawing room and inside the mind of the protagonist, Staff-Captain Riabovich.

The opening lines establish a properly realistic background; they read like a military report indicating the precise date (20 May) and time of evening (8:00 P.M.) when Riabovich's artillery brigade arrives at its bivouac. Yet no sooner has this specific information been given than the scene undergoes a transformation: "A rider in civilian dress, on a strange horse [*strannaia loshad'*] appeared from behind a church . . . the horse approached not directly but sideways, as it were, making little dancing movements as if it were being lashed on the legs." The horseman delivers a formal invitation to tea from retired general von Rabbek, and in a moment the rider and his strange horse disappear behind the church. "The devil knows what that means!" some of the officers exclaim. Though the officers may not be aware of the danger of invoking the devil by name, readers familiar with romantic literature may be certain that something extraordinary is about to take place.

The scene itself, with its unexpected arrival of the strange horseman, suggests an apparition such as are found in romantic tales from the 1830s. In every way it challenges the regulated nature of military life: the rider is in civilian dress, his strange horse seems undisciplined, and they both appear and disappear "from behind the church." The role of the church is at first puzzling; it is mentioned six times at the beginning, once in the middle, and four times at the end of the story. In a sense, it functions as a frame. And if we think of the dual nature of the church as a place of religious awe and simultaneously dark and mysterious, we may surmise that Chekhov intended it to occupy a place more significant than that of a mere landmark. The rider appears from behind the church, just as pagan forces lurk behind the fervor associated with charismatic believers. Thus the church may be either an ambiguous shield or a source of the mysterious rider.

In a similar way, the landscape is initially undistinguished but soon becomes suggestive of danger. The officers are told that they can reach von Rabbek's estate by one of two paths: "a lower one, going down behind the church to the river and then along the bank to the garden itself . . . or the upper one—straight from the church along the road which . . . leads to the master's barns." That the landscape seems to betray a kind of dual personality is suggested by its description: "At the first barn the road divided in two: one branch went straight ahead and disappeared in the evening mist, the other went to the right, to the master's house. . . . Stone barns with red roofs, heavy and sullen-looking, very like barracks in a district town, stretched along both sides of the road." ⟨. . .⟩

The landscape description as the officers leave the party seems ominous:

> . . . They went along the path which descended to the river and then ran along the edge of the water, bending around the shoreline bushes, pools, and the willows hanging above the water. The riverbank and path were barely visible, and the opposite bank was completely drowned in darkness. Here and there on the dark water were reflections of stars; they trembled and became scattered—and this was the only way that one could guess that the water ran swiftly. It was quiet. On the other bank sleepy sandpipers were moaning (*stonali*) but on this side, in one of the bushes, . . . a nightingale began to pour forth its call loudly. The officers stood next to the bush, touched it, but the nightingale kept on singing.

The threatening dark, the rushing water, the pitiful sound of the birds on the other side of the river, accompanied by the nightingale's insistent call (a warning sign in Slavic and European folklore), should give Riabovich reason for concern. He does not take notice of them, however; and the remainder of the story pulses between his romantic imagination and military routine.

The leitmotiv "strange," found first in the unusual invitation and the undisciplined horse, figures prominently in Riabovich's imagination as he longs for a repeat invitation. It returns to close the episode. When the unit passes by the von Rabbek estate once again, the river and its banks are the same as before, but there is no aroma of the trees and bushes; even the warning call of the nightingale is missing. The garden's former magic has evaporated, and Riabovich now thinks that it would indeed be strange if he were to meet his unknown woman again. As he approaches the river and watches the rivulets extend the moon's reflection and break it into pieces, his mood of resignation turns to one of despair. Watching the river's constant flow, he now recognizes the contrast between cyclical nature and individual human existence, which is destined never to be repeated. Summarizing his romantic experience and life itself, he exclaims: "How stupid. How stupid." This judgment demonstrates that his existential dilemma is significantly more profound than that of Verochka's Ognev, for Riabovich now perceives his life as "unusually barren, miserable, and colorless. . . ." Here the reader may remember his self-characterization as "colorless" (*bestsvetny*), a description that has a secondary suggestion of "flowerless." Riabovich has been unable to find his ideal, the unknown woman with whom he has spent the summer in imaginary wedded bliss. Was she perhaps the young lady in the lilac dress? If so, than he is indeed without his crowning flower.

—Joseph L. Conrad, "Vestiges of Romantic Gardens and Folklore Devils in Chekhov's 'Verochka,' 'The Kiss,' and 'The Black Monk,'" in *Critical Essays on Anton Chekhov*, Thomas A. Eekman, ed. (Boston: G. K. Hall & Co., 1989): pp. 81–82, 83–84.

RICHARD FREEBORN ON CHEKHOVIAN ESSENCE

[Richard Freeborn is the author of *Russian Literary Attitude: From Pushkin to Solzhenitsyn* (1976) and *Russian Revolutionary Novel: Turgenev to Pasternak* (1982). In this extract, taken from his introduction to *The Steppe and Other Stories* (1991), he comments on the Chekhovian essence of "The Kiss."]

Of the hundreds of stories which Chekhov wrote in the 1880s, none seems to capture the essence of the term 'Chekhovian' quite as brilliantly as *The Kiss*. It seems to have been written exceptionally quickly, perhaps over the space of a couple of days while Chekhov was staying in the hotel 'Moscow' in St. Petersburg after the production of his first play, *Ivanov*. The very speed of the composition may have helped to fix the story's meaning before it could lose its instantaneous freshness. It emphasizes superbly the eternally Chekhovian message that life's transience acts fatefully on human beings to alter forever their assumptions about themselves.

An artillery officer, Ryabovitch—"'I am the shyest, most modest, and most undistinguished officer in the whole brigade!'"—is invited to a party at the house of a local General. He accompanies his brother officers there, takes no part in any of the entertainments, but, losing his way in the darkened rooms, suddenly finds himself embraced by a woman and kissed. He has obviously been mistaken for someone else. The moment, though, permeated by the scents of lilac and roses, and the chilly tingling sensation like peppermint drops remaining on his skin from the kiss, permanently enchants him. He seems to have been caught in the thralls of a vague, inexpressible love that consumes him for the rest of his life.

Though the realities of an artilleryman's bivouac existence are suggested well enough, what is permanent, unchanging for him, his only guarantee against the everyday impermanence surrounding him, is the thought that, as a result of that moment, 'something extraordinary, foolish, but joyful and delightful, had come into his life.' The very vagueness of it can seem unsatisfactory. Chekhov ironically underscores the teasingly vague legacy of Ryabovitch's kiss by describing his ultimate disillusionment. The whole of life became for him, 'an unintelligible, aimless jest' over which he can be said to have had the last laugh. By deliberately ignoring the General's second invitation he snubbed his fate, as it were. The kiss tended to reverse his assumptions about himself, but in doing so it became vampiric.

—Richard Freeborn, Introduction to *The Steppe and Other Stories* (New York: Alfred A. Knopf, 1991): pp. xxv–xxvi.

[Ronald L. Johnson teaches writing and literature at Northern Michigan University. This extract is taken from his book *Anton Chekhov: A Study of the Short Fiction* (1993). Here he discusses Chekhov's common imagining of a "little man."]

This "impotence of soul" is an early example of a major concern of Chekhov: the inability of a person to overcome his isolation.

Within the year, Chekhov was to publish ⟨a⟩ story in which a man turns away from an experience that holds out promise of emotional fulfillment. The events in "The Kiss" revolve around the emotions of an ordinary man, a "little man," the quintessential Chekhovian hero. Ryabovitch, an artillery officer of common feelings and intelligence, is physically small in stature with sloping shoulders, spectacles, and lynxlike whiskers; his appearance suggests he is the "most undistinguished officer in the whole brigade." One evening at a party, Ryabovitch accidentally wanders into a dark room where an unknown woman clasps him in her arms and passionately kisses him. When the woman realizes he is not the man with whom she had an appointed rendezvous, she flees, her face unseen, and Ryabovitch experiences a new sensation, wanting "to dance, to talk, to run into the garden, to laugh out loud." He forgets his undistinguished appearance, and searches for the woman.

Although Ryabovitch cannot identify the woman, later at his quarters the thought of the kiss gives him an "intense groundless joy." He feels something "extraordinary, foolish, but joyful and delightful" has come into his life. When the brigade marches away to another district, he clings to this new agreeable thought to fight the boredom of his life. Ryabovitch considers himself an ordinary person, but now because of his dreams of a relationship with the woman, this ordinariness of his life "delighted him and gave him courage." At summer's end, Ryabovitch is assigned back to the district where the party occurred. But as he passes the house where the party was held, he feels his dreams were all simply imaginings, and nothing will ever come of them. At this point, the whole world seems an "unintelligible, aimless jest"; his own life in particular "struck him as extraordinarily meager, poverty-stricken, and colorless." Chekhov's artistic achievement in "The Kiss" lies first in making this common imagining of a "little man" so vividly convincing, so his mundane life swells with emotional richness; and second, in illustrating the humanness in his terrible disappointment when he achieves "true" perspective on his dreams. Ironically, the imagined experience leaves the "little man" finally poorer in spirit.

—Ronald L. Johnson, *Anton Chekhov: A Study of the Short Fiction* (New York: Twayne, 1993): pp. 26–27.

Plot Summary of
"Rothschild's Fiddle"

"Rothschild's Fiddle" was written in 1894. Its protagonist is Yakov, a seventy year old coffin maker who lives in a town "worse than a village" (Chekhov's simile) because, although it is inhabited by old people, they die so rarely that Yakov's business is not doing well. In the story, Yakov is sometimes nicknamed "Bronza."

Yakov's coffins are made solidly and strongly. The author tells us that he always measures his "customers," but is very reluctant to take orders for children's coffins. This detail, which is relayed in passing, will turn out to be of importance later on when the reader learns that Yakov had a child who had died some fifty years before. However, Yakov seems to have forgotten all about this loss; he is obsessed with losses of another kind: financial. He meticulously records in his ledger the value of the money that he might have earned, had people only died more often.

He lives poorly with his wife Martha, whom he doesn't treat with kindness. Besides coffin making, he also earns a living by playing the violin in the local Jewish orchestra. However, Yakov develops a hatred towards all Jews, especially towards the flutist Rothschild. After Yakov once almost beat Rothschild, the orchestra called him only when absolutely necessary.

One day, Martha suddenly falls ill, and we witness the change in his self-awareness. Triggered by the unusually bright and strangely happy expression on her face in the contemplation of her approaching death, he realizes that death will bring her relief from her unhappy life with him.

There follows a remarkably vivid scene in the hospital where Yakov, his wife, the doctor, and the doctor's assistant, are in direct conversation with each other. Yakov's humble servility doesn't help in persuading the doctor to show some concern for the poor woman. Probably seeing a hopeless case of typhoid fever, he discharges her with words that go beyond cruelty: "she has lived long enough." But Chekhov doesn't stop there: he unveils the dark power of inertia that has led Yakov all his life and leaves the reader speechless: When they return from the hospital, Martha stands for a long time next to the stove, afraid that if she lies down Yakov will start talking about his losses. At the same time Yakov is contemplating the approaching religious holidays when he will not be permitted to work, which means that the coffin will have to be made now. So, Yakov measures his wife with his iron yardstick, and begins working on the coffin. Chekhov adds a tinge of absurdity: When Yakov completes it, he writes his wife's name and the charges dutifully in his book of losses. The circle is complete: what he quotes as a gain (the charge for a coffin) is his loss (he pays out of his own money).

Martha asks her husband if he remembers the baby that God had given, then taken away, some fifty years before and how they used to sit under the willow tree on the bank of the river. Yakov cannot recall either the baby or the willow tree.

After his wife dies and is buried, Yakov is seized by a great distress. When he meets Rothschild on the street, he wants to beat him up again. As Rothschild runs away, the flutist is bitten by a dog and Yakov hears his despairing screams. He sits down on the bank of the river and the picture of a little child flashes across his memory, and he starts to think about life and death: "Why had Yakov brawled and wrangled all his life, why had he shouted and gone for people with his fists, ill-treated his wife, and, he wondered, for what earthly reason had he frightened and insulted that Jew the other day? Why do people in general hinder each other from living? What losses it causes! What terrible losses!" In his mind, Yakov adds his own unlived life to his book of losses.

Soon after this Yakov gets the same illness that killed his wife, and he knows he is going to die. This time the visit to the doctor is depicted in one paragraph.

The story comes to closure with Yakov playing the violin while thinking of his wasted life. Fearfully, his old enemy Rothschild comes in to ask him if Yakov will play in the orchestra for an expensive wedding. The change in Yakov is apparent in the gentle manner in which he address Rothschild—"Come on, don't be afraid"—and the way he treats his former enemy.

As he is dying, Yakov's last wish is for his fiddle to be given to Rothschild. The story ends with Rothschild playing a sad tune (the one Yakov played after becoming ill). He plays this melancholy music so well that it is constantly requested by the merchants and people of the town.

Dmitrii Merezhkóvsky, a Russian critic, may have had Yakov in mind when he wrote: "Chekhov heroes have no life, there is only the daily routine without any event, or with only one event—death, the end of being. Daily routine and death: there are the two fixed poles of Chekhov's world." ❀

List of Characters in
"Rothschild's Fiddle"

Yakov Ivanov, whose nickname is Bronza, is a coffin maker in a small town. Yakov is never in good humor because he constantly has to endure business losses. When his wife dies, however, he realizes that he can put his wasted, unlived life in his book of losses. But Yakov plays violin splendidly and his last wish is to give the violin to Rothschild.

Martha, Yakov's wife, is never addressed tenderly by her husband. Her death causes Yakov to rethink his own life.

Rothschild is a flutist in the local Jewish orchestra. He is described as a red-bearded man "with a network of red and blue veins on his face." He respects Yakov for his music but not for his personality. When he inherits Yakov's violin at the close of the story, he plays Yakov's tune so delightfully that the townspeople often make him play it ten times in succession. ❀

Critical Views on
"Rothschild's Fiddle"

ILYA EHRENBURG ON YAKOV'S HUMANITY

[Ilya Ehrenburg (1891–1967) was a distinguished Russian writer. His works included *Russia at War* (1943), *The Ninth Wave* (1955), *The Extraordinary Adventures of Julio Jurenito* (1958), and *The Second Day* (1984). In this extract, taken from his 1962 book *Chekhov, Stendhal and Other Essays*, he asserts the inner humanity of Yakov.]

In the story "Rothschild's Fiddle," the undertaker Yakov (who makes a little money on the side by playing the fiddle) when his wife falls ill takes her measurements with an iron footrule: he makes the coffin in advance. After his wife's death he sits by the river and is sad. 'He could not understand how it had come about that during the last forty or fifty years of his life he had never been by the river, or if he had, he had paid no attention to it. The river was a good one, not a mere stream; he might have started up a fishing business, and sold the fish to merchants, officials and the manager of the station buffet and then put the money in the bank . . . Why do people always do just what they shouldn't? Why had Yakov brawled and wrangled all his life, why had he shouted and gone for people with his fists, ill-treated his wife, and, he wondered, for what earthly reason had he frightened and insulted that Jew the other day? Why do people in general hinder each other from living? What losses it causes! What terrible losses!' What Yakov does is inhuman, but there is a human being alive inside him. He plays the fiddle with such melancholy that the Jewish musician he has offended weeps. But there is the word 'losses,' and this is what gives Yakov's remorse, his sorrow, his hopeless grief that reality which moves the reader to the core.

—Ilya Ehrenburg, *Chekhov, Stendhal and Other Essays*, Anna Bostock and Yvonne Kapp, trans. (London: MacGibbon and Kee, 1962): pp. 43–44.

IRINA KIRK ON LOSSES

[Irina Kirk is a professor of comparative literature and Russian literature at the University of Connecticut. Her works include *Profiles in Russian Resistance* (1975) and *Anton Chekhov* (1981), as well as a novel, *Born with the Dead* (1963). Here Kirk writes about the meaning of "loss" in "Rothschild's Fiddle."]

"Rothschild's Fiddle" (1894) describes the emotional poverty of the coffin-maker, Bronza, who can only define his life in terms of the losses he sustains. There is little joy or pleasure in Bronza's preoccupation with his financial deficit, yet he is firmly entrenched in the pattern of interpreting everything within this framework. As the title indicates, his violin and all the potentialities it embodies will ultimately assume a greater value to Bronza.

His wife's illness and subsequent death have the initial effect of temporarily shifting the coffin-maker's attention from his financial losses to his spiritual impotence. It's clear from her joy and eagerness to die that Marfa welcomes any sort of liberation from life with her husband. Bronza recalls that

> All his life he had never treated her kindly, never caressed her, never pitied her, never thought of buying her a kerchief for her head . . . but only roared at her, abused her for her losses, and rushed at her with shut fists . . . and now, beginning to understand why she had such a strange, enraptured face, he felt uncomfortable.

Another indication of Bronza's and Marfa's bleak life together is the old woman's lyrical recollection of their small, blond-haired daughter who died fifty years earlier. Bronza doesn't even remember his wife's description of the happy moments they spent together singing under the willows; rather he is preoccupied with the loss of the two rubles, forty kopecks which Marfa's coffin cost him.

It is only later, after Marfa has been buried with satisfying "honour, order and cheapness," that Bronza sits under the willow tree his wife had mentioned, and for the first time notices the loveliness of the river flowing by. At first he reckons its beauty in terms of profit and losses, estimating the river's possibilities for accruing wealth, but gradually the word "loss" is transferred to an aesthetic, spiritual level:

But look backward—nothing but losses, such losses that to think of them makes the blood run cold. And why cannot a man live without these losses? Why had the birch wood and the pine forest both been cut down? Why is the common pasture unused? Why do people do exactly what they ought not to do? Why did he all his life scream, roar, clench his fists, insult his wife? For what imaginable purpose did he frighten and insult the Jew? Why, indeed, do people prevent one another from living in peace? All these are also losses! Terrible losses! If it were not for hatred and malice people would draw from one another incalculable profits.

The following day Bronza is ill and knows that he will soon die. At this point the word "profit" ironically replaces "loss" as the verbal leitmotif: Bronza muses

that from death at least there would be one profit; it would no longer be necessary to eat, to drink, to pay taxes, or to injure others; and as a man lies in his grave not one year, but hundreds and thousands of years, the profit was enormous. The life of man was, in short, a loss, and only his death a profit.

Bronza thus does not regret the passing of his life, but rather life itself. He is filled with sorrow that everything beautiful in the world must decay, including his fiddle, the birch wood, and the pine forest, and in one of his few generous moments plays the fiddle with compassion for this life "full of losses." Bronza's redemption becomes complete when in a burst of good feeling, he wills the beloved fiddle to his former enemy, the Jew Rothschild.

But the story ends on an ironic note. After Bronza's death Rothschild has learned to imitate his sad melody that was inspired by pity for life's decay, and has turned it into an economic "gain." The last sentence draws attention to the materialistic pettiness that permeates life and which makes people deaf to its real meaning:

But this new song so pleases everyone in the town that wealthy traders and officials never fail to engage Rothschild for their social gatherings, and even force him to play it as many as ten times.

—Irina Kirk, *Anton Chekhov* (Boston: Twayne Publishers, 1981): pp. 95–97.

[Ronald L. Johnson teaches writing and literature at
Northern Michigan University. This extract is taken from
his book *Anton Chekhov: A Study of the Short Fiction* (1993).
Here he discusses Chekhov's compassionate attitude
towards his characters.]

The subject of the authentic life is also the theme of "Rothschild's
Fiddle." This highly focused short story is narrated by a voice
separate from the consciousness of the protagonist, a mode that
became pronounced in the stories during Chekhov's last period,
from 1895 to 1904. This masterpiece illustrates Chekhov's
compassionate attitude toward his characters as well as any story he
wrote. In contrast to "In Exile" and "Ward Number Six," the
protagonist in this story does not argue directly with an antagonist
but he does come to recognize the inauthentic nature of his life and
undergo a moral conversion, triggered by the death of his wife.

Jacob, a coffin maker, loses his wife of fifty years to typhoid fever.
After her funeral, he realizes how inhumanely he treated her during
their marriage, for it now seems he no more noticed her than he did
a "cat or dog." Through this portrayal of Jacob's awareness of his
indifference toward his wife, Chekhov generates sympathy for the
character. In his grief, Jacob wanders down to a river where he used
to spend time with his wife and daughter. This daughter had died in
a past so far removed from the present that he had forgotten her. On
the riverbank, Jacob has an epiphany in which he realizes his life had
"flowed past without profit, without enjoyment—gone aimlessly,
leaving nothing to show for it." Because of the inauthentic nature of
his past life, Jacob realizes that his "future was empty." He develops
an awareness of the humanness of people in which he not only
questions his ill treatment of his wife, but his mistreatment of a Jew
named Rothschild. Jacob, who occasionally plays the fiddle in a
Jewish band, is anti-Semitic, "obsessed with hatred and contempt for
Jews," and in particular, he despises Rothschild, whom he had
insulted before his walk down to the riverbank. But after this
epiphany, when Rothschild approaches him again, Jacob treats him
with compassion.

Shortly afterward, when Jacob himself is dying from typhoid fever,
he plays his fiddle with a great poignancy, a poignancy which

Rothschild is able to recapture afterwards in his own playing. At Jacob's death, his moral conversion complete, he leaves Rothschild his fiddle in a gesture that symbolizes the compassion that has developed out of his suffering. Charles May observes that Chekhov's pathos in this story is set in an objective, ironically comic mode closely resembling the tales of Bernard Malamud.

—Ronald L. Johnson, *Anton Chekhov: A Study of the Short Fiction* (New York: Twayne Publishers, 1993): pp. 66–67.

Plot Summary of
"The Student"

Chekhov wrote the short story "The Student" (originally titled "In the Evening") at Yalta in 1894. In a conversation with the writer Ivan Bunin, he described it not only as his favorite among all his works, but also as a manifesto in favor of optimism. That statement still baffles his readers and literary critics.

The opening lines describe the gloomy weather in the winter. Chekhov anthropomorphises nature: "the thrushes were calling," "in the swamps close by something alive droned pitifully with a sound like blowing an empty bottle."

A theological student, 22-year-old Ivan Velikopolsky, is walking home on Good Friday after a shooting expedition. The feeling of pessimism is easily created: the cold weather, thoughts of his parents' poverty and hunger. And here Chekhov does something unexpected: the narration follows an unbroken thread of misery back through the history of Russia, from Rurik, the first ruler (A.D. 862–879), to the time of Ivan the Terrible and Peter the Great. The desperate poverty has existed for the past thousand years and will not change in the next following.

At that moment, Velikopolsky approaches the gardens of the widows Vasilisa and her daughter Lukerya. Standing next to their bonfire, the recollection of the Apostle Peter's renunciation of Christ comes spontaneously to Ivan's mind. "At just such a fire the Apostle Peter warmed himself. . . . So, it must have been cold then, too. . . . "

What follows is a story-within-the-story.

Ivan tells the biblical story of the Last Supper when Peter told Jesus that he was ready to go with him into darkness and unto death, but Jesus answered: "I say thee, Peter, before the cock croweth thou wilt have denied me thrice." And so, Peter's soul turned out to be weak and weary, and though he loved Jesus passionately, he denounced him before the High Priest. When the next morning the cock crowed, Peter remembered the words of Jesus, and began to weep bitterly.

Vasilisa is also moved to tears. Ivan realizes that "the old woman wept, not because he could tell the story touchingly, but because Peter was nearer to her, because her whole being was interested in what is passing in Peter's soul."

Immediately after, the transitory moment comes: instead of being bereft of hope at the awesome universal tragedy of Peter's betrayal, a joy suddenly stirs in his soul. There is a link between past and present, and as he leaves the women, and crosses the river on the ferry boat, he apprehends that truth and beauty have always existed and guided human lives, and the "feeling of youth, health and vigor, and the expectations of happiness looked to him enchanting." Despite suffering and tragedy, despite denials and betrayals, despite broken illusions of oneself and others, hope and belief are still stronger than despair. ❀

List of Characters in
"The Student"

Ivan Velikopolsky, a 22-year-old theological student, is the son of a sacristan. Although he is surrounded by poverty, after telling the story of St. Peter's denunciation of Christ he is overwhelmed by an irrational urge to think that truth and beauty have always guided human life.

Vasilisa is a widow who lives in poverty with her daughter and who is moved to tears after hearing the student's story of Peter's betrayal of Christ. She is described as a tall, fat old woman wearing a man's coat. She is the woman of experience and knows to express herself with refinement. The smile never leaves her face.

Lukerya is Vasilisa's daughter, also a widow. The author pictures her as "a little pockmarked woman with a stupid-looking face, whose husband used to beat her." ❀

Critical Views on
"The Student"

DONALD RAYFIELD ON THE CYCLICAL SHAPE OF
THE STORY

[Donald Rayfield is a professor of Russian at Queen Mary and Westfield College, University of London, where he has taught for more than thirty years. He is the author of the monumental 1998 biography *Anton Chekhov: A Life,* and of numerous publications, including *The Cherry Orchard: Catastrophe and Comedy* (1994) and *Understanding Chekhov: A Critical Study of Chekhov's Prose and Drama* (1999). This extract is taken from his book *Chekhov: The Evolution of His Art* (1975). Here he argues that the narration of suffering, like religion, gives meaning to life.]

The Student is an oddity among the Melikhovo works, but technically it is among the most representative in Chekhov's *oeuvre.* At the outset Chekhov very precisely establishes time and place, the visual and auditory impressions on the hero, and leaves vague all the traditional details of his face and gait. Nature is given predominance. Even in such a brief work, changes of mood are initiated by nature: the weather suddenly becomes wintry, thrushes and snipe call, something croaks in the marshes, slivers of ice appear in the river. These images lead to a series of apparently unrelated phenomena: a shot, a sound like someone blowing over an empty bottle, all bring a sense of desolation and hollowness to the hero, whose name, like all those in late Chekhov, is perfectly convincing and yet also links him with the open countryside through which he is passing: he is Velikopol'sky, 'great fields.' The fragmentary background given—the coughing father, the bare-footed mother, the student's hunger—integrates him all the more closely into the scene. As he approaches the two widows to whom he is to tell the story of Peter's betrayal, the verbs of the narrative already prefigure tension, conflict: the verb *dulo, dul* (blew) shows the disturbance in nature and in the hero; the paradox of the hero's fingers frozen stiff (*zakocheneli*) while his face is burnt (*razgorelos'*) by the wind anticipates the strange mixture of misery and joy in his story and the reaction to it.

The most striking element of the structure is its cyclic shape: all the details of the scene are mirrored in the story of Peter's betrayal, which in turn is mirrored in the final page of narrative. The workmen on the other side of the river correspond to the workmen warming themselves by the fire in the story of Peter: the calling of the birds in the opening phrases corresponds to the triple crowing of the cock; the description of the younger widow as *zabitaya* (beaten down) corresponds to the description of Christ, beaten and tormented (*bili, zamuchennyy*); the weeping of Peter (*zaplakal* and the Church Slavonic *plakasya*) leads to the weeping of Vasilisa. The campfire in the story of Peter is echoed by a campfire in the background of the last scene; the dawn of Peter's betrayal corresponds to the sunset into which the student walks. On one level, this structure merely shows how a natural scene—desolate spring, a camp-fire, two widows—provokes a narrative which embodies its mood and its details. But two paragraphs, at the beginning and the end of the story, show us how Velikopol'sky's thoughts make more of the connection. The word *dul* (blew) inspires the student with the thought that 'now' is part of eternity, that this scene of poverty is, like the wind, timeless. From that idea of dejection spring the narrative and the final joy of the whole story: if want and wind are timeless, so are the great moments of human suffering. And if these moments are meaningful to later generations, then art, the narration of suffering, like religion, is meaningful. Rarely was Chekhov's integrated imagery so economically effective. The final paragraph of the story is typical in its symbolism of his ecclesiastical works. The overjoyed student crosses the river by the ferry: as in *On Easter Eve* of 1886 and elsewhere, the river symbolises the division of two worlds. He climbs a hill and looks down on his village—a moment of transfiguration, of escape from the prison of environment, again to be seen in *In the Ravine* when Lipa walks on the hillside above her village. The images of sunset and daybreak, with their blood-red coloring, remain ominous, but in *The Student* the association of Peter and the present day makes the 'coldness' insignificant: the final impressions are of truth, beauty and happiness.

The rhythm of the language brings out the joy of the student's narration. The first part of the story is harsh and laconic; when the student begins to speak, the style becomes rich and gentle. Some of his language is childlike: his double adjectives, *tikhiy-tikhiy, tyomnyy-tyomnyy, gor'ko-gor'ko* (quiet, dark, bitter). Some is exotic, his Church Slavonic *petal* (cock), *vecherya* (last supper), *plakasya* (he wept), mingling the past with the present in the very texture of the prose. The last part of the story has a verbal rhythm that follows the movement of the characters. 'Vasilisa suddenly sobbed (*vskhlipnula*), tears, big, copious' is punctuated to show the convulsions of tears. The third paragraph from the end of the story is cast as a Tolstoyan series of syllogisms, slow, firm and dry: 'If Vasilisa cried . . . then clearly, what he had just been relating . . . was relevant to the present . . . and probably to this empty village, to himself, to everyone. If . . . then not because . . . but because . . . and because . . . in what had been happening.' Almost without concrete imagery, with a stringent syntax unlike that of the rest of the story, this paragraph mimics the tortuous, even clumsy cerebral reaction in Velikopol'sky. If we compare this 'cerebral' passage, with its conjunctions and its parallel constructions, with the last paragraph, we can see the difference between thought and intuition. The last paragraph is one lone sentence of a hundred words, one flow of images concrete and abstract, moving from 'the ferry . . . river . . . hill . . . village . . . sunset' to 'truth . . . beauty . . . youth . . . health . . . strength . . . joy . . . sense.' There is no 'because': the construction is parenthetic, not logical, and is made when 'when,' 'where,' 'he thought about how'; with dashes, with 'and's, leading not to an elucidation, but to a climax. The third paragraph from the close explains what has happened; the last paragraph is a subjective ending. For Chekhov the illusion of an imminent break-through of happiness was in his last words more important than the verifiable observations on the present. *The Student* is a perfect example in miniature of Chekhov's art, and it bridges the gap between the ecstatic mood of the ecclesiastical and steppe stories of 1886 and 1887 and the lyricism of the prose of the 1900s.

—Donald Rayfield, "The Student" from *Chekhov: The Evolution of His Art* (London: Paul Elek, 1975): pp. 153–55.

[David W. Martin is a professor at the University College of Swansea. In this extract he discusses factual material from the Gospels that Chekhov used in *The Student*.]

Chekhov's story shows a fine structural balance, and the student's account of Peter's denial of Christ constitutes its pivotal point, the point at which the hero's feelings begin to undergo their striking metamorphosis. It is his account that forms the particular subject of this investigation. The investigation pays special attention to any inaccuracies which may be found in Chekhov's handling of the biblical sources at his disposal, whilst at the same time providing a general commentary on his use of them in the story, whether or not discrepancies in *realia* occur.

The sight of the fire, then, reminds Velikopol'skii of the night of Peter's denial of Christ and prompts him to ask Vasilisa a question: "You have most likely been to the reading of the Twelve Gospels?"

Here the student is referring to a particular service of the Eastern Orthodox Church. The service is technically Mattins for Good Friday, although it is invariably held on the Thursday evening of Holy Week. During the service are read out twelve New Testament passages which relate to Christ's arrest and death. The actual passages read do not vary from year to year and were fixed before the conversion of Russia to Christianity in the tenth century. Velikopol'skii describes only those events which are covered by the first three Gospel readings, so only they are of relevance to this note. They are as follows: (1) John 13. 31–18.1. (2) John 18. 1–28. (3) Matthew 26. 57–75.

In answer to the student's question Vasilisa says that she has been to the service mentioned. He then sets about reminding her of what she has heard there concerning Peter's denial of Christ. His use of phrases such as "if you recall" or "you heard" gives the impression that he bases his account not on general knowledge of the events of the New Testament, but specifically on the texts of the Twelve Gospels read out in Holy Week.

He begins:

> If you recall, during the Last Supper Peter said to Jesus: "I am ready to go with thee both into prison and unto death."

These words are quoted by Velikopol'skii from the Gospel according to St. Luke, 22. 33. They are not, in fact, read out in the service which ostensibly supplies the student with his reason for reminding the woman of them. The equivalent passage read at the church service is John 13. 37:

> Peter said unto him, Lord, why cannot I follow thee now? I will lay down my life for thy sake.

Even at the start of Velikopol'skii's account, then, Chekhov is not concerned accurately to reflect the service that the student is purportedly describing. The woman would not remember the quotation that he tries to draw to her attention.

Velikopol'skii continues:

> And at this the Lord said to him: "I tell thee, Peter, the cock . . . shall not crow this day before that thou shalt thrice deny that thou knowest me."

These words are, again, taken from Luke (22. 34), a passage not read out at the service described. There, the scene is presented in St. John's account (John 13. 38):

> Jesus answered him, Wilt thou lay down thy life for my sake? Verily, I say unto thee, The cock shall not crow, till thou hast denied me thrice.

Whilst the differences in wording here between Luke and John are evident enough, there is, in the Church Slavonic version used in the Russian Church, a further distinction between them, one of relevance to the present theme. The student, in explaining the scene to Vasilisa, quite naturally first uses the Slavic work for cock (πετεη), as found in the biblical passage he is citing. Then, apparently supposing the woman will not have understood the word when it was read out in church, he gives the modern Russian equivalent (*to est'petukh*—the omission of this phrase in the quotation above is indicated). This detail lends a necessary touch of warmth to the student's characterization, which could easily have lost its spontaneity amid verbatim quotations from the New Testament. However, whilst the word πετεη does indeed occur in the Church Slavic version of Luke's account, John here uses a word of Greek extraction: *alektor*. This, then, is the word Vasilisa would have heard in church, and it would have been more true to reality had Velikopol'skii explained *alektor* to her, and not *petel*. 〈. . .〉

From what has been said above one may draw the following conclusions. First, that the student's account of Peter's denial of Christ, and of the events leading up to it, is of a dual nature, in that it shows a fairly strict adherence to the story as it is told in the Gospel according to St. Luke (suggesting that Chekhov actually referred to that Gospel in writing the work), whilst at the same time it is interspersed with the student's personal reflections which serve to add a spontaneity and warmth which would be lacking in a virtually literatim reproduction of the Bible text. Mention has been made in this connection of Velikopol'skii's thoughts on Peter's state of mind on the night in question and of his visualization of Peter weeping in the darkness.

Secondly, Chekhov's use in the manner described in St. Luke's Gospel shows a definite preference for it over the passages from the New Testament, describing the same events, which are read out at the service of the Twelve Gospels. Because the student refers to this service, it would have been more logical to base the account on those passages from John and Matthew which are read at it. One may surmise that this was not done because Luke in a number of instances presents the events in a more dramatic form. Peter's assertion that he would follow Christ "both into prison and to death" is more appealing from a purely literary point of view than the equivalent passage in John ("I will lay down my life for thy sake"). Christ's state of mind in the Garden of Gethsemane, the kiss that Judas gives Christ, the glance that passes between Christ and Peter—none of these things figure in the church service, but all are eminently suited to the deliberately emotional tone of Chekhov's story.

The third and final point which should be stressed is that, although the student is, of course, at liberty to relate the story of Peter's denial of Christ according to whichever Gospel he chooses, when he specifically refers to the service of the Twelve Gospels and then misrepresents it, as is the case in a number of instances described above, we are then confronted with discrepancies in the field of *realia*. Derman is surely correct in his assertion that Chekhov was in general careful not to allow such discrepancies into his work. Whilst it would be possible to assert that he was prepared to so on this occasion in order to show lack of knowledge on Velikopol'skii's part and characterize him, therefore, as a poor student, such a conclusion would be somewhat recherché and secondary to the notion that St. Luke's Gospel was found to be more suited to the atmosphere of heightened emotion that Chekhov was eager—even at the cost of inaccuracy—to maintain throughout the student's account.

—David W. Martin, "*Realia* and Chekhov's 'The Student,'" *Canadian-American Slavic Studies* 12, no. 2 (Summer 1978): pp. 268–70, 273.

✍

L. M. O'TOOLE ON POINT OF VIEW

[L. M. O'Toole is the author of *Structure, Style and Interpretation in the Russian Short Story* (1982). In this chapter he discusses the point of view and character in the story.]

It all depends on the point of view. The slightest unexpected shift of focus may create irony. A consistency of point of view will tend to strengthen a particular atmosphere.

Ever since Percy Lubbock's examination of this particular problem of novel structure in *The Craft of Fiction*, a majority of critics and literary theorists have assumed that the application of a closed-ended label, such as 'first person narrator,' 'third person, omniscient,' would be an adequate substitute for analysis of point of view. But these labels provide only the broadest indication of what we need to know. At least three-quarters of Chekhov's stories use the 'third person, limited omniscient' point of view which has been neatly defined as follows: 'The author narrates the story in the third person, but chooses one character as his 'sentient center' whom he follows throughout the action, restricting the reader to the field of vision and range of knowledge of that character alone.' But how much more is learnt about one of these stories by applying this label? The necessary information is not who held the camera, but his angle and distance from the subject at any particular moment, his 'aperture' (receptiveness), 'focus' (clarity of vision) and 'shutter speed' (intelligence). The author may adjust any of these at different points in the story and the pattern of his adjustments will probably bear some relation to the pattern of elements in the narrative structure.

A careful examination of the opening paragraph of *The Student* will show that this is not just a piece of objective description of nature providing the setting for the story. 'At first' and 'when it grew dark' show an awareness of the passing of time. 'Nearby,' 'in the marshes,' 'in the wood,' 'from the east' and 'across the lakes' show an awareness of position in relation to the surrounding world. The sounds: 'sand,' 'moaned,' 'rang out,' 'fell silent' and the physical sensations: 'a penetrating cold wind began to blow', 'inhospitable,' 'remote,' are apprehended by a specific human consciousness which, moreover, responds emotionally to this rather threatening world with a mournful image and highly subjective words such as 'plaintively,' 'boomingly,' 'merrily,' 'inopportunely,' 'empty of people.' With the steady growth in emotional intensity through a so far anonymous point of view, by the end of the paragraph with its despairingly brief final sentence: 'It smelt of winter,' the identification and characterisation of this human consciousness becomes an urgent necessity. Chekhov has fulfilled Poe's requirement that from the very first sentence everything should tend to the outbringing of the preconceived effect.

In the second paragraph a single sentence tells, from the narrator's objective point of view, all the facts of the student's biography and present situation that are vital for the story, but which could not convincingly or economically be presented through his musings or recollections. From this point forward everything is revealed via the consciousness of the character whom Chekhov has chosen to embody in the story's title: physical sensations, visual impressions, memories, historical and philosophical thoughts; moods and emotions. Since the theme and the peripeteia of the story concern the change that takes place in the student's own psyche when he sees how his audience reacts, it is important that the characterisation of the two widows is conveyed through his appraisal of their appearances, gestures and speech. Vasilisa's deferential smile and Luker'ya's stupid, unwavering stare are revealed, as shall be shown, through the student's consciousness. The awesome universal tragedy of Peter's betrayal is given immediacy and a human scale through the student's comments and explanations. As already seen, the vision of history as a chain, the touching of one end of which will stir a response at the other end, is the student's own. It does not matter that the image is unoriginal (the student is an interpretative rather than a creative artist); what matters is the force of the student's realisation of this truth. The dénouement and epilogue, matching the prologue and complication, are bound by the whole logic of the story to be the product of the student's point of view. The atmosphere of the story depends partly on the tension and interplay between the student's awareness of himself and his awareness of the world around him, between his present and his past, between the clear focus of his immediate surroundings, the blurred focus at the edges and the darkness of what lies beyond. The lens-angle angle widens and narrows like a zoom device. There is a consistency of atmosphere in *The Student* because there is a consistent point of view.

As has often been pointed out, the choice of 'third person, limited omniscient' point of view enables an author to combine the virtues of subjectivity (an authentic and deeply felt emotional response) and objectivity (the power to analyse and generalise). That the 'sentient centre' of this point of view coincides with the consciousness in which the story's essential reversal takes place, strengthens in *The Student* the two prime virtues of short-story form—unity and economy.

The foregoing examination of plot and point of view leaves little need for a detailed analysis of the creation and function of *character* in the story. As already seen, knowledge of the student is built up from a complex pattern of sensations, visual impressions, memories, thoughts, emotions, gestures and language. Because of his central function in theme, plot and narrative structure, it is important that he has strong sensations, a sense of history and a sense of justice, that he can pity as well as criticise. As a student of theology he knows the Good Friday story almost by heart, as a humane person he can be moved by the affective power of the tragedy, as an intellectual he can rationalise this power, and as an idealist he can gain hope from his rationalisations.

As has been noted, the most effective aspect of the characterisation of the two widows is their juxtaposition. Vasilisa's height and girth and presence contrast with Luker'ya's littleness, ugliness and subjugation; the one knows the world and the gentry and has learned a little of the arts of social hypocrisy, the other is limited in outlook and unresponsive; the one responds actively, the other with mute passivity. The reader, like the student, has some contact with and sympathy for Vasilisa, and yet, by a nice paradox which Chekhov clearly engineered, it is the very negativity of Luker'ya's emotional reaction which is moving:

her expression became heavy, strained, like that of someone stifling severe pain.

Luker'ya is unaffected by physical discomfort and pain: could it be that Peter's tragedy and resulting grief give her more pain than anybody? Chekhov strengthens the atmosphere of the story by leaving the reader to decide.

—L. M. O'Toole, "Chekhov's 'The Student,'" in *The Structural Analysis of Russian Narrative Fiction*, Joe Andrew, ed. (Staffordshire, England: Keele University, 1984): pp. 12–14.

ROBERT LOUIS JACKSON ON THE AFFIRMATION OF LIFE IN THE STORY

[Robert Louis Jackson is B. E. Bensinger Professor of Slavic Languages and Literature at Yale University. He is also President of the International Chekhov Society. His numerous writings include *The Art of Dostoevsky: Deliriums and Nocturnes* (1981), *Reading Chekhov's Text* (1993), and *Dialogues with Dostoevsky: The Overwhelming Questions* (1996), as well as essays on Turgenev, Gogol, Chekhov, Dostoevsky, and Tolstoy. In this essay, Jackson writes about the real heroes in the story "The Student."]

"The student thought again that if Vasilisa had shed tears, and her daughter had been troubled, it was evident that what he had just been telling them about, which had happened nineteen centuries ago, had a relation to the present—to both women, to the desolate village, to himself, to all people. The old woman wept, not because he could tell the story touchingly, but because Peter was near to her, because her whole being was interested in what was passing in Peter's soul." It is noteworthy that the old woman not only feels a connection with Peter but that she feels it with "her whole being." These words echo Mark 12:30–33: "And thou shalt love the Lord thy God with all thy heart, and with all thy soul, and with all thy mind, and with all thy strength. . . . And to love him with all the heart, and with all the understanding, and with all the soul, and with all the strength, and to love his neighbor as himself, is more than all whole burnt offerings and sacrifices."

What is important is that these women experience the suffering of Peter and the Passion of Christ with their entire being. Chekhov's thought is clear: One's commitment to one's fellow man, to the good, to God, cannot be abstract, "from a distance." It cannot be conditional or based on the expectations of returns, results, payment. It must be unconditional, total, above all deeply felt, that is, experienced with one's entire being, with all the heart.

At this point it is appropriate to ask: Who are the real heroes of Chekhov's story? The answer is clear: not the student, not Peter, but the women. Vasilisa and her daughter are the real heroes of the story, in the same way that Russian women have always been the real heroes of Russian life and literature, be they simple peasants or aristocratic wives of Decembrists. Vasilisa and her daughter are the heroes because in the most essential terms of human experience they have kept the faith: theirs is the light of the biblical "burning bush," and they have kept the fires burning. The women have nursed and nourished the children, served family and life; they have tended the garden, worked, endured the hardest labor; they have done the work of men as well as of women; and through it all they have maintained their humanity and image. Chekhov describes Vasilisa this way: "A tall, fat old woman in a man's coat was standing by and looking thoughtfully into the fire. . . . [She] expressed herself with refinement, and a soft, sedate smile never left her face." One may recall at this point some remarks by Dostoevsky in a little essay in *Diary of a Writer* entitled "On Love for the People: A Necessary Contract with the People." Dostoevsky writes: "One has to be able to separate out the beauty in the Russian belonging to the common people from the alluvial barbarism. Owing to circumstances, almost throughout the whole history of Russia, our people has been to such an extent subjected to debauchery and to such an extent corrupted, seduced, and constantly tortured that it is still amazing how it has survived, preserved its human image, not to speak of its beauty. Yet it preserved the beauty of its image as well."

Vasilisa experiences the story of the suffering of Peter and of Jesus with "her whole being." These words prelude a qualitative change in Ivan's whole being: "And joy suddenly stirred in his soul, and he even stopped for a minute to take a breath." No detail is without meaning in Chekhov's great masterpieces. The Russian phrase for "to take a breath" is *perevesti dukh*. *Perevesti* means "to transfer," "move," "shift"; *dukh* is here, idiomatically, "breath," but in its main meaning it is also "spirit," that same *dukh* that is hidden away in *vzdokhnul*, as was noted earlier. One may say, then, that in both a literal and a figurative sense a transfer of the spirit takes place in Ivan; in other words, he experiences the paschal transfiguration. Indeed, according to the Gospels, Jesus "yielded up the ghost" (in Russian, *ispustil dukh*) (Matthew 27:50) but was "quickened by the Spirit" (*ozhil dukhom*) (I Peter 3:18) and was resurrected by the Divine Spirit. Such is the character of the paschal change that takes place in Ivan.

Ivan's grief and self-pity have been overcome through a deeply felt ethics of connection—through relating to people and life. Ivan's deep breath, his spiritual crossing over, leads immediately to often-quoted lines from Chekhov's "The Student," lines that articulate the central theme of connections in the story: "The past, he thought, is linked with the present by an unbroken chain of events flowing one out of another. And is seemed to him that he had just seen both ends of that chain; that when he touched one end the other quivered."

Ivan is filled with a sense of renewal. He now crosses the river in a boat—the moment is full of rich symbolism—and mounts the hill from which he looks out on "his village and towards the west where the cold crimson sunset lay in a narrow streak of light." There Ivan "thought that truth and beauty which had guided human life there in the garden and in the yard of the high priest had continued without interruption to this day, and had evidently always been the chief thing in human life and in all earthly life, indeed; and the feeling of youth, health, vigor—he was only twenty-two—and the inexpressible sweet expectation of happiness, of unknown mysterious happiness, took possession of him little by little, and life seemed to him enchanting, marvellous, and full of lofty meaning."

Ivan experiences the paschal transfiguration in a moment that seems to allude to Jesus' ascent to the mount. The life that had seemed senseless and unchanging to Ivan but a short while ago as he made his way homeward is now full of "lofty meaning." Ivan looks to the west, upon his village, and upon the crimson sunset with an expectation of happiness. There is an allusion in this final scene not only to Jesus' ascent to the mount but also to that moment when Moses on Mount Nebo looked west to the promised land and the

Lord declared: "I have caused thee to see it with thine eyes, but thou shalt not go over thither" (Deuteronomy 34:4). Like Moses, Ivan will not see the promised land on earth: like Peter, he, too, will surely experience new trials and tribulations. What is important, though, is his sustaining vision, a profoundly ethical one, of "truth and beauty."

Relevant here are some words of A. A. Bogolepov on the significance of Easter: "Easter is the triumph of trampled truth and beauty. Granted—not in all fullness; granted—only in part; nonetheless, truth is attainable also on this earth. Granted—not always; granted—only at times, but it can be victorious even here. This faith has moved people."

—Robert Louis Jackson, "Chekhov's 'The Student,'" in *Reading Chekhov's Text*, Robert Louis Jackson, ed. (Evanston, Ill.: Northwestern University Press: 1993): pp. 130–32.

Plot Summary of
"The Darling"

When "The Darling" first appeared in print in 1899, several critics thought that Chekhov wrote the story to mock dependent women, and they blamed his character Olenka (the Darling) for her submissiveness. Even Chekhov's friends were divided: where Gorky opposed the story and thought of Olenka as a "gentle slave," Tolstoy saw Olenka's character as an embodiment of feminity: "The soul of Darling, with her capacity for devoting herself with her whole being to the one she loves, is not ridiculous but wonderful and holy."

The original title in Russian is "Duschechka" which is diminutive of the word "soul," the precious one.

The story opens with Olenka sitting on her back porch, and Kukin, the manager of the open-air theater, complaining about the weather. For three successive days Olenka listens to Kukin's laments about the state of affairs of the theater, his artists, and the town. Somehow his misfortunes, the author tells us, touch her and she begins to love him.

While he is described as a small thin man, yellowish in his complexion, with "an expression of despair on his face," she is depicted as a quiet, soft-hearted girl with rosy cheeks, tender eyes, and plump shoulders. Chekhov discusses her quality of giving, and explains that she has always been fond of someone and couldn't exist without loving.

Olenka marries Kukin and they get on well together. The theater becomes the center of her life as it is her husband's. She echoes Kukin's words about the new theater productions that the public likes or dislikes.

In her marriage she beams with satisfaction while Kukin grows thinner and yellower, perpetually bewailing the losses. At the beginning of the spring he goes to Moscow to assemble a new troupe, but he suddenly dies there. For three months Olenka is in deep mourning, sobbing so loudly in her house that the neighbors can hear it.

But then, one day on her way back from church, she meets Pustovalov, a timber merchant, who eventually proposes to her. After their wedding, Olenka and Pustovalov live in harmony for six years, during which time she once again becomes fully absorbed in her husband's interests and ideas.

When Pustovalov is away on a business trip, a young veterinarian Smirnin, who is separated from his wife, comes and keeps Olenka company. Then Pustovalov catches cold suddenly and dies. For six months, we are told, Olenka leads the life of a nun. All of a sudden, her comment on the state of affairs in the veterinary vocation reveals her attachment to the other man. For the third time, Chekhov has her echo her man's convictions, but hastily adds that no one could judge her harshly, since everything she does comes so naturally.

This happiness doesn't last for long. Smirnin is transferred to Siberia and Olenka is left alone and adrift. She gets thinner and plainer, and her mental and emotional emptiness are concisely captured: "She looked into her yard without interest, thought of nothing, wished for nothing, and afterwards, when night came on she went to bed and dreamed of her empty yard" and compared it with the taste of wormwood in the mouth.

After years have passed, during which she incessantly feels her empty, dreary, and bitter soul, one July day Smirnin arrives in town with his wife and son. Olenka unselfishly offers them her house, without asking for rent, and she moves to the lodge. Shortly afterwards, Smirnin's wife leaves and the little boy, Sasha, is entrusted to Olenka's care. Right away, with splendid devotion so characteristic of her, Olenka takes the little boy's opinion on the school's program as her own. Still in the author's exclamation, "Ah, how she loved him! Of her former attachments not one had been so deep, never had her soul surrendered to any feeling so spontaneously, so disinterestedly, and so joyously as now that her maternal instincts were aroused," we feel a touch of irony, because we know for certain that she loved her father, her French teacher, and her two husbands with all her soul, expecting nothing in return. Is Chekhov being ambivalent towards his heroine, as Tolstoy thought?

In his afterword to the story, Tolstoy observes that Chekhov "intended to damn, but the God of poetry forbade him to do so and ordered him to bless, and he blessed and unwillingly clothed this dear creature in such wondrous light that it forever will remain an example of what a woman can be in order to be happy and to make happy those with whom fate brings her." He further remarks: "This story is so excellent because it came out unconsciously." ❀

List of Characters in
"The Darling"

Olga Semyonovna, Olenka, "Darling" has all her life been fond of someone and could not exist without loving. She marries twice and twice she devotes herself completely to her husband. The same happens in her relationships with the veterinary surgeon and with his son.

Kukin is Olenka's first husband. Being the manager of an open-air theater he constantly worries about the weather. He is a small thin man with a yellow complexion. An expression of despair never leaves his face. He goes to Moscow to assemble a troupe for the theater, but suddenly dies.

Pustovalov is Olenka's second husband. Although he is in the timber trade, Pustovalov looks more like a country gentleman. He and Olenka get on well for six years, until he catches cold one winter and dies.

Smirnin is a young veterinary surgeon, married but separated from his wife, with whom he has a little boy. When Olenka, on one occasion, gets involved in the conversation with his fellow veterinary surgeons, he is so embarrassed that when the guests are gone, he yells at her angrily.

Sasha is Smirnin's son, a boy of ten, with blue eyes and dimples in his cheek. His mother leaves him with Olenka, who becomes deeply attached to him. ✾

Critical Views on
"The Darling"

RENATTO POGGIOLI ON LOVE IN THE STORY

[Renatto Poggioli was the author of *Poets of Russia: 1890–1930* (1960), *Spirit of the Letter: Essays in European Literature* (1965), and *Theory of Avant-Garde* (1968). This extract focuses on love, Olenka, and Tolstoy's interpretation of the story.]

One may wonder whether Tolstoy is equally right in identifying the motive that had led the author of *The Darling* to take the pen. "When Chekhov began to write that story," says Tolstoy, "he wanted to show what woman ought not to be." In short, what Chekhov meant to do was to reassert his belief in the ideal of woman's emancipation, in her right and duty to have a mind and a soul of her own. While acknowledging the artistic miracle which had turned a satirical vignette into a noble human image, Tolstoy seems to enjoy as a good joke the implication that the author had to throw his beliefs overboard in the process. Being strongly adverse to the cause of woman's emancipation, Tolstoy speaks here *pro domo sua*, but the reader has no compelling reason to prefer his anti-feminism to Chekhov's feminism. Tolstoy has an axe to grind, and his guess is too shrewd. One could venture to say that Chekhov sat down to write *The Darling* with neither polemical intentions nor ideological pretensions: what he wanted to do was perhaps to exploit again at the lowest level a commonplace type and a stock comic situation, which, however unexpectedly, develops into a vision of beauty and truth. If D. S. Mirsky is right in claiming that each Chekhov story follows a curve, then there is no tale where the curve of his art better overshoots its mark.

What must have attracted Chekhov was the idea of rewriting a half pathetic, half mocking version of the "merry widow" motif: of portraying in his own inimitable way the conventional character of the woman ready and willing to marry a new husband as soon as she has buried the preceding one. That such was the case may still be proved through many eloquent clues. No reader of *The Darling* will fail to notice that Olenka calls her successive mates with almost identical nicknames: Vanichka the first, Vassichka the second, and Volodichka the third. These familiar diminutives, although respectively deriving from such different names as Ivan, Vasili, and Vladimir, sound as if they were practically interchangeable, as if to suggest that the three men are interchangeable too.

This runs true to type, since in the life scheme of the eternal, and eternally remarrying, widow, nothing really changes, while everything recurs: the bridal veil alternates regularly with the veil of mourning, and both may be worn in the same church. It is from this scheme that Chekhov derives the idea of the successive adoption, on Olenka's part, of the opinions and views of each one of her three men, and this detail is another proof that the story was originally conceived on the merry widow motif. Yet, if we look deeper, we realize that a merry widow does not look for happiness beyond wedded bliss: that she asks for no less than a ring, while offering nothing more than her hand. But Olenka gives and takes other, very different things. She receives her husbands' opinions, and makes them her own, while returning something far more solid and valuable in exchange. And when she loses the person she loves, she has no more use for his views, or for any views at all.

This cracks the merry widow pattern, which begins to break when she joins her third mate, who is a married man, without a wedding ceremony or the blessing of the Church. And the pattern visibly crumbles at the end, when Olenka finds her fourth and last love not in a man, but in a child, who is the son of her last friend. "Of her former attachments," says Chekhov, "not one had been so deep." Now we finally know Olenka for what she really is, and we better appraise in retrospect some of the story's earliest, unconscious hints. Now, for instance, we understand better her girlish infatuations for such unlikely objects as her father, her aunt, or her teacher of French. For her, almost any kind of person or any kind of love can do equally well, and it is because of this, not because of any old-maidish strain, that she fails to reduce love to sex alone.

Chekhov explains this better than we could, at that very point of the tale when the lonely Olenka is about to find her more lasting attachment: "She wanted a love that would absorb her whole being, and whole soul and reason—that could give her ideas and an object in life, and would warm her old blood." For all this one could never say of Olenka, as of Madame Bovary, that she is in love with love: she cares only for living beings like herself, as shown by the ease with which she forgets all her husbands after their deaths. Her brain is never haunted by dreams or ghosts, and this is why it is either empty, or full of other people's thoughts. This does not mean that the "Darling" is a parrot or a monkey in woman's dress, although it is almost certain that Chekhov conceived her initially in such a form. She is more like the ass of Balaam, who sees the angel his master is unable to see. Olenka is poor in spirit and pure in heart, and this is why life curses her three times, only to bless her forever, at the end.

Tolstoy is right when he reminds us that, unlike Olenka, her three men and even her foster-child are slightly ridiculous characters, and one must add that they remain unchangingly so from whatever standpoint we may look. The reminder is necessary: after all, the point of the story is that love is a grace proceeding from the lover's fullness of heart, not from the beloved's attractive qualities or high deserts. In the light of this, the parallel with Balaam's ass must be qualified by saying that Olenka sees angels where others see only men. Thus the double message of the story is that love is a matter of both blindness and insight. ⟨. . .⟩

D. H. Lawrence recommends that we never trust the writer, but only the tale. This is what one should do even with Chekhov, although he is one of the most trustworthy of modern writers, precisely because he builds on a broad moral structure, which compensates for the restrictions of his chosen literary forms. If this is true, then one must reject Leo Shestov's statement that Chekhov's is a creation *ex nihilo*, always returning to the nothingness from which is sprang forth. It would be more proper to define it a creation *ex parvo*, producing from humble beginnings a somber and yet beautiful world.

—Renatto Poggioli, "Storytelling in a Double Key" in *Anton Chekhov's Short Stories*, Ralph E. Matlaw, ed. (New York: W. W. Norton, 1979): pp. 324–26, 327–28.

Thomas G. Winner on Mythological Allusions in the Story

[Thomas G. Winner is the author of *Oral Art and Literature of the Kazakhs of Russian Central Asia* (1958) and *Chekhov and His Prose* (1966), from which this extract is taken. In it he discusses the relationship of "The Darling" to the myth of Eros and Psyche.]

During the last years of Chekhov's life a certain change in his viewpoint can be noted. After the trilogy and "Ionych," which represent the fullest expression of Chekhov's concern with man's destruction by *pošlost'*, we find a somewhat more optimistic tone in some stories written after 1898, as well as in the major plays, which were all written after 1896.

The three stories which express most clearly the mood of Chekhov's later years are "The Darling" (*Dušečka*, 1898), "The Lady with the Pet Dog" (*Dama s sobačkoj*, 1899), and the last of Chekhov's stories, "The Betrothed," (*Nevesta*, 1903). While all three stories are concerned with man's isolation, a qualified hope is expressed concerning man's ability to find a certain happiness. Yet, lest we be tempted to oversimplify trends in Chekhov's final years, it should be remembered that during this period Chekhov also wrote the last of his milieu stories, "In the Ravine" (1900), which although it ended with an assertion of humaneness, also provided a strong picture of man's brutality. ⟨. . .⟩

The picture of Olenka, devoid of a personality of her own, lacking inner resources and entirely dependent on others, on whom she thrusts her love, is partly a satirical one. But "The Darling" is not only the story of an empty human being; and whether or not one agrees with all the implications of the Tolstoyan view that Olenka is, in the end, not ridiculous but even "holy," this interpretation cannot be overlooked. While it appears at first that Olenka may become one of Chekhov's typical figures of emptiness and hypocrisy, the fact that she is capable of love, even though it is submissive and possessive, distinguishes her from many Chekhovian lonely protagonists. Tolstoy's position, however, that in the elevation of the submissive Olenka, Chekhov was rejecting, although not consciously, his earlier ideas of woman's emancipation, is hard to justify. For Olenka's absurdity cannot be overlooked. Her naïve identification with anyone willing to accept her love, and her immature personality, which is only a reflection of others', contribute to ridicule, rather than to an idealization of woman's maternal role. Olenka's idealization of those she loves, when contrasted to an objective depiction of these persons, is also comic. 〈. . .〉

We note again in this story the implication of literary or mythological allusions. The relationship of "The Darling" to the myth of Eros and Psyche has been discussed by Renato Poggioli, who sees Chekhov's story as a modern version of the myth, "as a furtive hint that even in the profane prose of life there may lie hidden poetry's sacred spark." The ironic implications of the parallel with the myth are, however, not noted by Poggioli. It will be recalled that Apuleius, recounts the story of Psyche, loved by the god Eros who appears only at night and forbids her to look upon him. When Psyche breaks the command of Eros and secretly gazes upon her sleeping lover, the god immediately vanishes. Poggioli noted that Chekhov's heroine, Olenka, is called *dušečka*, an endearing expression similar to "darling," which is also the diminutive form for the Russian word *duša*, soul. Psyche, the heroine of the myth, is also named for the Greek word for soul. Thus the pet name of Chekhov's heroine, which is the title of his story, hints at the ancient myth.

Like Psyche, Olenka loves blindly. Unlike Psyche, however, she is not forced by curiosity to inspect those she loves. Poggioli, in the spirit of Tolstoy's criticism, writes that Olenka realized unconsciously what Psyche failed to understand: that love is blind and must remain so. But is Olenka a wiser version of Psyche, as Poggioli implies, or an ironic reflection? Those whom Olenka loves successively are but absurd shadows of the god of love. Had Chekhov's Olenka held a light to her lovers, as did Psyche to Eros, Olenka's lovers might also have vanished. It was, however, their prosaic attributes, not their godlike qualities, which could not bear close inspection. Thus Olenka and her lovers are again examples of lowered versions of a myth. The echo of the myth in the characterization of Olenka provides more than a romantic suggestion of the artless wisdom of Olenka's unquestioning love. For it also suggests that Chekhov's Olenka, who must retain her illusions, is too naïve to see or doubt.

—Thomas G. Winner, *Chekhov and His Prose* (New York: Holt, Rinehart and Winston, 1966): pp. 209–10, 211–12, 215–16.

[In this extract, taken from her 1977 book *Chekhov: A Study of the Major Stories and Plays*, Beverly Hahn describes the transferences of Olenka's love.]

The ending of the story, where the little boy upon whom 'the darling' now concentrates her love cries out in his sleep—'I'll give it you! Get away! Shut up!'—certainly suggests an intention to judge; and so does the ironic exaggeration throughout of Olenka's own emptiness of opinions and total transference of interests along with her transferences of affection. But the source of the irony also becomes a source of delight and the comedy gradually outweighs the judgment:

> It was evident that she could not live a year without some attachment, and had found new happiness in the lodge. In anyone else this would have been censured, but no one could think ill of Olenka; everything she did was so natural. Neither she nor the veterinary surgeon said anything to other people of the change in their relations, and tried, indeed, to conceal it, but without success, for Olenka could not keep a secret. When he had visitors, men serving in his regiment, and she poured out tea or served the supper, she would begin talking of the cattle plague, of the foot and mouth disease, and of the municipal slaughter-houses.

In the context—after so many easy transferences of love—the 'everything she did was so natural' is obviously uneasy in its sympathies. Yet its sarcastic echo cannot survive the humour of Olenka's talking of the foot and mouth disease, a humour which immediately expands the reader's tolerance. Without going so far as to say, as Tolstoy does, that Olenka emerges as an ideal of devoted womanhood, one can surely agree with the outline of his response:

> In spite of its exquisite gay humour, I at least cannot read without tears some passages of this wonderful story. I am touched by the description of her complete devotion and love for Kukin and all that he cares for, and for the timber merchant and for the veterinary surgeon, and even more of her sufferings when she is left alone and has no one to love; and finally the account of how with all the strength of womanly, motherly feelings (of which she has no experience in her own life) she devotes herself with boundless love to the future man, the schoolboy in the big cap.

It is indeed a 'wonderful' story in the sense that that word expresses one's affection for it. Yet the sources of its pathos are relatively facile, and it does not really advance our understanding of women beyond the understanding reached in the earlier stories. The reason for this is not that what Chekhov embodies in Olenka is unpalatable as a psychological truth—we probably recognize some truth in the portrait, at least in relation to some women—but that Olenka is an embodiment of a proposition rather than a real character. She embodies one possible aspect of womanhood, singled out and exaggerated; if we recognize her and respond to her, it is still, I think, not with complete belief.

—Beverly Hahn, *Chekhov: A Study of the Major Stories and Plays* (Cambridge: Cambridge University Press, 1977): pp. 230–32.

☙

IRINA KIRK ON OLENKA'S CHILDLIKE IDENTITY

[Irina Kirk is a professor of comparative literature and Russian literature at the University of Connecticut. Her works include *Profiles in Russian Resistance* (1975) and *Anton Chekhov* (1981), as well as a novel, *Born with the Dead* (1963). In this extract Kirk writes about Olenka's total surrender to love.]

The opening paragraph of "The Darling," in which Olenka is introduced to the reader, is constructed with a combination of details that immediately draw attention to her childlike identity. It is first established that she is the daughter of a retired collegiate assessor, and although it is mentioned that Olenka is "deep in thought," the next sentence explains that these thoughts are only about the relief evening will bring from flies and the heat.

The next paragraph introduces Olenka's future husband Kukin, the despairing manager of a local theater, whom she loves with pity and maternal solicitude. Kukin's attraction to Olenka appears to be directed more toward her plump good looks than toward an appreciation of her devotion to him. "He proposed to her, and they married. And when he had a good look at her neck and her plump, firm shoulders, he struck his hands together, and exclaimed, 'Darling!'" The romanticism of Kukin's feelings toward Olenka is further undercut by his mood after the wedding: "He was happy, but as it rained on their wedding day and the night that followed, the expression of despair did not leave his face."

In fact, although it is clearly stated that Olenka and her new husband "got on well together," it is also mentioned that "Olenka was gaining weight and beamed with happiness, but Kukin was getting thinner and more sallow and complained of terrible losses, although business was fairly good." These two statements are not mutually exclusive as they might appear to be at first glance: Olenka's maternal solicitude only encourages her husband's indulgent self-pity, and thus her love becomes fatal to him.

Chekhov's deliberately comic wording of the telegram informing Olenka of Kukin's death foreshadows his attitude toward her subsequent behavior: "Ivan Petrovich died suddenly today awaiting prot instructions funnyral Tuesday." The misspelled word "funnyral," in Russian *Pokhorony*, has associations with laughter, and the incomprehensible word *prot* adds to the absurdity of the telegram. Olenka proceeds to sob folk laments ("My precious! Why did we ever meet? Why did I get to know you and to love you?"), dresses in black, and after three months of grief marries again after a two-day romance.

Olenka's second husband Pustovalov impresses her as appearing "more like a landowner than a business man." She respects him for his substantial appearance and for his fatherly advice to her that "if one of our dear ones passes on, then it means that this was the will of God, and in that case we must keep ourselves in hand and bear it submissively." Her marriage to him is every bit as satisfying to Olenka as the relationship she had and cherished with Kukin: she becomes involved with Pustovalov's lumber business to the same degree that she had earlier devoted herself to Kukin's theater, she adopts her new husband's "sedate and reasonable manner" with the same abandon that she had earlier responded to Kukin's emotionalism, and she is equally bereaved when after six years of marriage to Pustovalov, he suddenly dies.

Again there follows a period of mourning in Olenka's life, this time lasting six months, which is characterized by the same folk laments and by the black clothing she donned after Kukin's death. Yet when Olenka begins to talk only of the veterinary business, and is seen happily doting on her veterinary boarder, it is clear that she has found another lover to give meaning to life. But unlike her first two husbands "Volodichka" resents her total identification with him and admonishes her, "I've asked you before not to talk about things that you don't understand. When veterinarians speak among themselves please don't butt in! It's really annoying!" Olenka's "happiness" with the veterinary does not last long in any case: he is transferred away with his regiment and she is left totally abandoned.

Yet Olenka arrives at perhaps her most perfect fulfillment in life when the veterinary returns and leaves his small son Sasha in her care:

> She now had opinions of her own . . . saying that studying in high school was hard on the children, but that nevertheless the classical course was better than the scientific one because a classical education opened all careers to you . . . How she loves him! Not one of her former attachments was so deep; never had her soul surrendered itself so unreservedly, . . . and with such joy as now when her maternal instinct was increasingly asserting itself. For this little boy who was not her own . . . she would have laid down her life . . . with tears of tenderness. Why? But who knows why?

There is an intimation that Olenka's total surrender to her love for Sasha will be her final undoing. Her domination over the boy is constantly threatened by the return of his mother, and from the last line of the story it is evident that the boy himself has dreams of rebellion. Olenka's doting love stifles Sasha, who sometimes expresses those emotions of independence in his sleep that will later be directed toward Olenka: "I'll give it to you! Scram! No fighting!"

—Irina Kirk, *Anton Chekhov* (Boston: Twayne Publishers, 1981): pp. 112–14.

⊗

SVETLANA EVDOKIMOVA ON OLENKA AND ECHO

[Svetlana Evdokimova is the author of *Pushkin's Historical Imagination* (1999). In this essay she compares Olenka's story to that of Echo's.]

Olenka's story, like Echo's, follows a sequence of births and deaths. Olenka is reborn each time she has the opportunity to merge her life with someone else's and to repeat someone else's "word." And Olenka dies an intellectual and spiritual death whenever she is deprived of that opportunity, losing all capacity for judgment and opinion. Like Echo, who shrivels up in the rocky caves after being spurned by Narcissus, Olenka withers away in her empty courtyard when her loves die or leave her: "Now she really was alone. . . . She got thinner; she lost her looks. And the passersby in the street would no longer look at her, as they used to before, and would no longer smile at her. . . . She would gaze blankly at her empty yard. She would think of nothing. She would want nothing. And afterward, when night came, she would go to bed and would dream of her empty yard. She would eat and drink as if against her will."

By contrast, in those moments when Olenka is full of love, she physically fills out as well: "Looking at her full [*polnye*] rosy cheeks, her soft white neck with a dark mole on it . . . men thought, 'Yes, you'll do!'" After Olenka's marriage to Kukin, her fullness (*polnota*) is stressed again: "He feasted his eyes on that neck and those plump [*polnye*], healthy shoulders." During this marriage, the narrator notes, "Olenka grew fuller [*polnela*] and beamed with happiness." And when Olenka finds her last love in Sashenka, she is described again as "a tall, stout [*polnaia*] woman."

The opposition full-thin (*polnyi-khudoi*) is further developed in the story into the opposition full-empty (*polnyi-pustoi*). In "The Darling," emptiness and thinness are observed to accompany the periods of Olenka's spiritual emptiness and solitude: "When she was with Kukin and Pustovalov, and later with the veterinary surgeon, Olenka could explain everything, and she would give her opinion on any possible subject, but now her mind and her heart were as empty as her yard." Love for the little boy brings Olenka back to life, once again inspiring her with opinions "after so many years of silence and emptiness [*pustoty*] in her thoughts."

Yet Olenka's fullness turns out to be ambiguous. When Smirnin reappears, bringing his son with him, Olenka's empty courtyard, a metaphor for her soul, is filled with dust: "On a hot July day, toward the evening, when the town herd of cattle was being driven along the street and the whole yard was filled [*napolnilsia*] with dust clouds, someone suddenly knocked at the gate." These dust clouds will inevitably dissipate, though, and the courtyard will become empty again. Likewise Olenka's fullness is always temporary. It is, in fact, itself a cloud of dust. She is doomed to stay forever empty in her empty yard, waiting for someone to come and to give her fullness of being, if only for a brief moment. Such is the fate of the Greek nymph Echo, hiding in hollow caves and waiting for those she can echo in order to become Echo, that is, in order to exist at all.

Given the typological similarity between the Darling and Echo, one can understand why Chekhov's story generated such contradictory responses from its readers. For the myth of Echo itself engendered different and often contradictory interpretations, in part because, in addition to the canonical and better-known tale of Echo and Narcissus discussed above, there exists a distinctly different version of the myth—the tale of Echo and Pan. In this tale, recounted in Longus's *Daphnis and Chloe,* Echo is a wood nymph and an excellent musician. She is a virgin who avoids the company of all males. Pan becomes angry with her because she rejects his advances and because he envies her musical skills. He therefore takes revenge on her by sending shepherds to rip her body apart. The pieces of Echo's body are then flung all across the earth, but they still sing and imitate all sounds as the nymph did before. "Pan himself they imitate too when he plays on the pipe," says Longus in his account of the myth.

Whereas the myth of Echo and Narcissus centers on Echo's reverberative sounds and repetitive language, the fable of Echo and Pan emphasizes the musical and, therefore, creative aspect of Echo. Hence two strands of interpretation—one positive and one negative—derive from the two conceptualizations of this figure. As John Hollander points out in his book *The Figure of Echo,* "in general it is in the milieu of Pan that Echo becomes a credential voice, associated with truth." It is this tradition, then, that led to the adoption of Echo as the symbol of poetry itself. By contrast, the negative readings of Echo arise from Echo's hollowness and repetitiveness, the qualities associated with the other Echo, the spurned lover of Narcissus. Thus Hollander concludes, "Pan's Echo is lyric, Narcissus' is satiric."

The ambiguity of Olenka's character and the differences among its interpreters lie precisely in that Olenka can be seen as both a satiric and a poetic character. The story, indeed, contains both lyrical and satiric overtones. As one Chekhov scholar has noted, as the end of the story the narrator's tone shifts from the satiric to the lyrical, as, for example, in the following passage: "For this little boy, to whom she was not related in any way, for the dimples in his cheeks, for his school cap, she would have given her whole life; she would have given it gladly and with tears of tenderness. Why? Who can tell why?" Here the narrator's irony gives way to lyrical pathos.

—Svetlana Evdokimova, "'The Darling': Femininity Scorned and Desired" in *Reading Chekhov's Text*, Robert Louis Jackson, ed. (Evanston, Ill.: Northwestern University Press: 1993): pp. 193–95.

⊕

DONALD RAYFIELD ON CHEKHOV'S PASSION FOR LIFE

[Donald Rayfield is a professor of Russian at Queen Mary and Westfield College, University of London, where he has taught for more than thirty years. He is the author of the monumental 1998 biography *Anton Chekhov: A Life*, and of numerous publications, including *Chekhov: The Evolution of His Art* (1975), *The Cherry Orchard: Catastrophe and Comedy* (1994), and *Understanding Chekhov: A Critical Study of Chekhov's Prose and Drama* (1999). In this extract he argues that changes in Chekhov's morality can be ascribed to the dying writer's passion for life.]

Chekhov's 'Dushecka' ('Darling,' 1898) was an ideal which the young Tolstaia and her father were proud to acknowledge. Printed in a popular journal, *Sem'ia* (*The Family*), the story seems a sudden conversion to the bourgeois ideal, and was greeted by reactionaries such as the elderly novelist Vasilii Nemirovich-Danchenko as enthusiastically as by anti-feminist radicals like Tolstoy. The story reverts to Chekhov's earlier comic technique: the succession of men who rule Olenka, the Darling's, life are caricatures: a theatre impresario, a timber dealer, a veterinary surgeon and a schoolboy, and her succession of bereavements and consolations make for a vaudeville narrative. The fundamental idea is that Olenka can have no interests and no ideas except those that she absorbs from the man she loves, whether it is the man who taught her French when she was a schoolgirl, or the schoolboy whose lunch she packs when she is an elderly woman. Olenka sees no disruption between the years when she lives for her first husband's theatre or her second husband's timber trade. She is a loving, instinctive chameleon. Nearly all Chekhov's readers took the story to be an ideal, or a reality. The narrative tone, while it has a warmth and simplicity missing from other work of the period, does however imply authorial perplexity about female nature. 'The Darling,' with her endurance of bereavement and childlessness, is a comic version of the tragedy of Lipa in 'In the Ravine.' What is different is the implication that the female is meant to be constant, to survive, and the male to be transitory, and to die. For his own times, and for Soviet times too, 'The Darling' created a standard for woman to be judged by. 'Dushechka' thus renewed the image of 'Dushen'ka' ('Little Psyche'), created out of La Fontaine by the poet Ippolit Bogdanovich more than a century previously, as a model of female self-sacrifice and love. By changing a consonant, Chekhov demoted the female ideal from the mythological to the bourgeois.

Changes in Chekhov's morality can be ascribed to the consumptive's passion for life. The Dreyfus affair had already germinated Chekhov's inbuilt distrust of all authoritarianism and his attachment to individual freedom. One other important factor affects Chekhov's work from 1899 to his death. He had finally sold the rights to his *Collected Works* for 75,000 roubles, to the publisher of 'My Life,' Adolf Marks, a hard-headed businessman who imposed stringent conditions. The most important was that Chekhov himself should retrieve and prepare all his earlier work for reprinting. 'That will keep Mr Chekhov busy,' remarked Marks. Being, as he half joked, a Marxist, meant that Chekhov had to devote his declining energy to revision, not original writing—which partly explains why his last four years produced just two plays and a handful of stories. While he rejected much of his earlier work, time was spent rewriting (largely cutting) earlier work and, above all, in considering how material he had failed (in his opinion) to realise fully, could now be recycled. The romantic situations and the heroines of his work for *New Times* in 1886, the figure of the doctor and the lawyer, the theme of the ruined estate, the artist as priest—all these themes are exhumed by a re-reading of earlier work.

Certainly Chekhov's abnegation of sensual enjoyment which tinges 'Three Years' has entirely gone by 1897. Lying on his back, in Ward No. 16 of the clinic in Moscow in spring '97, the author of 'Ward No. 6' had much to reflect on. Tolstoy visited him; their arguments led to a severe haemorrhage, but Chekhov managed to make Tolstoy define his ideas of divinity and immortality. Tolstoy said he looked on the afterlife as an embodiment of pure reason and pure love into which human souls would merge. To Tolstoy's amazement, Chekhov was repelled and perplexed by this Kantian transcendence of the individual. He rejected an afterlife in favour of a more fervently enjoyed mortality.

We find, about this time, in Chekhov's notebooks a new affirmation of agnosticism, of the right not to know, which seems to push him further away from Tolstoy: 'A good man's indifference is as good as any other religion. . . . Between "God exists and God does not exist" lies an enormous field. . . .' Chekhov now seems to wish to remain in the verdant pastures of this field, not to cross it, as he accuses Russian intellectuals, from one extremity to the other. Suddenly, in Chekhov's world death is less fearsome than a wasted life: just as the peasant Lipa is to realise that 'you only live once,' so Chekhov's doctors, lawyers, bankers and teachers are to stumble on the truth that happiness lies in grasping opportunities, in acting on desire, in letting the individual blossom to the full before it has to fade. The 'new, beautiful life' of the future goes on luring and bewitching the hero, but it no longer matters whether the 'new life' is real or illusory, so long as it works as a myth to stimulate the hero, or heroine, to act. The first thing we notice in Chekhov's last stories is the proliferation of verbs such as 'it seemed to him,' he calmed himself with the thought,' 'he was thinking.' The narrator's viewpoint has collapsed; once there is no certainty of right and wrong, the hero freely lets his instincts and impulses lead him on.

—Donald Rayfield, *Understanding Chekhov: A Critical Study of Chekhov's Prose and Drama* (Madison: University of Wisconsin Press, 1999): pp. 198–200.

Plot Summary of
"The Lady with the Dog"

The best known of Chekhov's works, "The Lady with the Dog" was written between October and December 1899. It is composed of four brief chapters, each not more than four or five pages long.

The opening sentence provides a full picture of a Crimean summer resort, Yalta, with its idle atmosphere and people looking for adventure. Gurov, the protagonist of this story, is a man who has been married since his second year of university, who hasn't reached forty, and who has a 12-year-old daughter. His wife is a woman with a solid frame who looks twice her age, has thick eyebrows, and likes to call herself "the woman who thinks." The author hastens to tell the reader that Gurov finds his wife unattractive and narrow-minded, and that he dislikes being at home. He conducts many affairs and has developed a general opinion of women as "the lower breed." (This echoes Nietzsche's conviction that "woman is created for the warrior's recreation.") With light irony, Chekhov informs us that without this "lower breed" Gurov couldn't exist.

Gurov enjoys every affair at its beginning, but each eventually bores him. He easily forgets about his bad experiences, however; "the desire for life surged in him," and he would fall again for an attractive woman.

In a restaurant, Gurov notices the woman seated at the table next to him. He begins his conquest by calling to the little dog and the link between him and her is established. Gurov turns out to be quite witty and he learns her name, Anna Sergeyevna, and that she grew up in Petersburg, got married and now lives in the city of S—. Through Gurov's recalling Anna's beautiful gray eyes and long neck Chekhov gives visible features of his heroine.

The second section of the story begins a week later, as Gurov and Anna are sitting together on the terrace of the restaurant. The day is hot and windy, and the air is dusty. In the evening, they go to the pier to watch the steamer. Chekhov subtly builds an atmosphere of tension and expectation, which culminates after the steamer arrives, when Gurov asks Anna where she would like to go. Anna doesn't answer, so Gurov kisses her, then fearfully looks around to see if anyone has noticed him.

After they become lovers in her hotel room, she regards herself as a fallen woman to whom Gurov will show no respect. Gurov, on the other hand, is bored by this reaction and eats watermelon for a half-hour while she cries. That scene over with, Gurov and Anna walk together around Yalta and sit on a bench looking at the sea. The leaves do not stir on the trees, the crickets chirp, and the monotonous muffled sound of the sea compares the peaceful day to the "eternal sleep awaiting us."

After several days, Anna Sergeyevna has to return to her town. After seeing her off, Gurov heads back north, to Moscow.

In the third section, Gurov returns to his life in Moscow: family affairs, the dinners at clubs, banquets, and celebrations. But he cannot forget Anna Sergeyevna; the memories are too overwhelming and he feels a strong desire to share them with someone. He is tired of his wife and children, of his job at the bank, and of his friends; his whole existence seems futile and dull. In December, using business as an excuse, he sets off for the town where the lady with the dog lives. He doesn't know why, but he wants to see Anna Sergeyevna again.

He takes the finest room in a fashionable hotel in the city of S—, and from the hotel porter he finds out the name of Anna's street. Relying on chance that he will meet her, Gurov wanders around town and stops at her house. The familiar little dog comes out, but Gurov's heart beats so violently that he can't remember its name. He decides to go to the premiere of *The Geisha Girl* in the local theater, where he sees Anna. He succeeds in talking to her during the intermission and convices her to meet him. She promises him she will join him in Moscow.

In the final chapter, Anna and Gurov are preparing for a secret meeting in Moscow. As soon as Anna arrives, she sends a messenger to Gurov. Both of them are leading double lives, one false (the outer one), and the important one, essential to them—the secret one.

During their meeting, Anna cries about their impossible relationship "from her bitter consciousness of the sadness of their life." Intending to calm Anna, Gurov caresses her, but catches sight of himself in the mirror. It strikes him that his hair is growing gray and that age is catching up with him, but that he has never loved until now. They begin to talk about how to free themselves from the contingencies of their respective existence, and they feel they are just at the beginning.

The uncertain future of Anna and Gurov is left unresolved. Originally Chekhov wrote in the conclusion of the story that love "made them both better." He altered it later on to "changed them both for the better." Finally, he changed it once again to "had changed them both," thus avoiding any moral. ❀

List of Characters in
"The Lady with the Dog"

Dmitri Dmitrich Gurov has not yet reached forty. He regards his wife as shallow and narrow-minded and is constantly unfaithful to her. A compulsive philanderer, he seduces Anna Sergeyevna while he is vacationing in Yalta, but when they part, her memory begins to haunt him.

Anna Sergeyevna is a young, inexperienced, decent woman who just recently has left boarding school in St. Petersburg. She has been married for about two years, but, when asked, she doesn't know what exactly her husband's job is. After Gurov seduces her, she thinks of herself as a fallen woman. ❀

Critical Views on
"The Lady with the Dog"

D. S. MIRSKY ON CHEKHOV, TOLSTOY, AND
DOSTOYEVSKY

[D. S. Mirsky was a Russian literary historian whose works
included *Pushkin* (1926), *A History of Russia* (1927), and
Russia: A Social History (1931). He occupied a unique
position as an interpreter of English literature to his
countrymen, publishing, for example, a book entitled *The
Intelligentsia of Great Britain* (1935). In this selection from
A History of Russian Literature (1926) he discusses the
differences between the art of Tolstoy, Dostoyevsky, and
Chekhov.]

Chékhov's art has been called psychological, but it is psychological
in a very different sense from Tolstóy's, Dostoyévsky's, or Marcel
Proust's. No writer excels him in conveying the mutual
unsurpassable isolation of human beings and the impossibility of
understanding each other. This idea forms the core of almost every
one of his stories, but, in spite of this, Chékhov's characters are
singularly lacking in individual personality. Personality is absent
from his stories. His characters all speak (within class limits and
apart from the little tricks of catchwords he lends them from time to
time) the same language, which is Chékhov's own. They cannot be
recognized, as Tolstóy's and Dostoyévsky's can, by the mere *sound of
their voices*. They are all alike, all made of the same material—"the
common stuff of humanity"—and in this sense Chékhov is the most
"democratic," the most "unanimist," of all writers. For of course the
similarity of all his men and women is not a sign of weakness—it is
the expression of his fundamental intuition of life as a homogeneous
matter but cut out into watertight compartments by the
phenomenon of individuality. Like Stendhal and the French
classicists, and unlike Tolstóy, Dostoyévsky, and Proust, Chékhov is a
student of "man in general." But unlike the classicists, and like
Proust, he fixes his attention on the infinitesimals, the "pinpricks"
and "straws" of the soul. Stendhal deals in psychological "whole
numbers." He traces the major, conscious, creative lines of psychical
life. Chékhov concentrates on the "differentials" of mind, its minor,

unconscious, involuntary, destructive, and dissolvent forces. As art, Chékhov's method is active—more active than, for instance, Proust's, for it is based on a stricter and more conscious *choice* of material and a more complicated and elaborate disposition of it. But as "outlook," as "philosophy," it is profoundly passive and "non-resistant," for it is a surrender to the "micro-organisms," of the soul, to its destructive microbes. Hence the general impressions produced by the whole of Chékhov's work that he had a cult for inefficiency and weakness. For Chékhov has no other way of displaying his sympathy with his characters than to show in detail the process of their submission to their microbes. The strong man who does not succumb in the struggle, or who does not experience it, is always treated by Chékhov with less sympathy and comes out as the "villain of the play"—in so far as the word "villain" is at all applicable to the world Chékhov moves in. The strong man in this world of his is merely the insensate brute, with a skin thick enough not to feel the "pinpricks," which are the only important thing in life. Chékhov's art is constructive. But the construction he uses is not a narrative construction—it might rather be called musical; not, however, in the sense that his prose is melodious, for it is not. But his method of constructing a story is akin to the method used in music. His stories are at once fluid and precise. The lines along which he builds them are very complicated curves, but they have been calculated with the utmost precision. A story by him is a series of points marking out with precision the lines discerned by him in the tangled web of consciousness. Chékhov excels in the art of tracing the first stages of an emotional process; in indicating those first symptoms of a deviation when to the general eye, and to the conscious eye of the subject in question, the nascent curve still seems to coincide with a straight line. An infinitesimal touch, which at first hardly arrests the reader's attention, gives a hint at the direction the story is going to take. It is then repeated as a leitmotiv, and at each repetition the true equation of the curve becomes more apparent, and it ends by shooting away in a direction very different from that of the original straight line. Such stories as *The Teacher of Literature, Iónych,* and *The Lady with the Dog* are perfect examples of such emotional curves. The straight line, for instance, in *Iónych* is the doctor's love for Mlle Túrkin; the curve, his subsidence into the egoistical complacency of a successful provincial career. In *The Teacher of Literature* the straight line is again the hero's love; the curve, his dormant dissatisfaction with selfish happiness and his intellectual ambition. In *The Lady with the Dog* the straight line is the hero's attitude towards his affair with the lady as a trivial and passing intrigue; the curve, his overwhelming and all-pervading love for her. In most of Chékhov's stories these constructive lines are complicated by a rich and mellow atmosphere, which he produced by the abundance of emotionally significant detail. The effect is poetical, even lyrical: as in a lyric, it is not interest in the development that the reader feels, but "infection" by the poet's mood. Chékhov's stories are lyrical monoliths; they cannot be dissected into episodes, for every episode is strictly conditioned by the whole and is without significance apart from it. In architectural unity Chékhov surpasses all Russian writers of the realistic age. Only in Púshkin and Lérmontov do we find an equal or superior gift of design. Chékhov thought Lérmontov's *Tamán* was the best short story every written, and this partiality was well founded. *Tamán* forestalled Chékhov's method of lyrical construction. Only its air is colder and clearer than the mild and mellow "autumnal" atmosphere of Chékhov's world.

—D. S. Mirsky, *A History of Russian Literature* (New York: Alfred A. Knopf, 1926): pp. 361–63.

VIRGINIA LLEWELLYN SMITH ON THE ENDING OF THE STORY

[Virginia Llewellyn Smith is the author of *Anton Chekhov and The Lady with the Dog* (1973), from which this extract is taken. Here, she asserts that Chekhov's work requires of the reader a certain degree of involvement and discusses the ambiguous ending of "The Lady with the Dog."]

The situation, indeed the entire plot of "The Lady with the Dog," is obvious, even banal, and its merit as a work of art lies in the artistry with which Chekhov has preserved in the story a balance between the poetic and the prosaic, and in the careful characterization, dependent upon the use of half-tones. Soviet critics have a valid point when they regard Gurov as a sort of Everyman; "The Lady with the Dog" is an essentially simple exposition of a commonplace theme. Unlike in "The Duel" and "Three Years," in "The Lady with the Dog" Chekhov has made no attempt to investigate the problems of love: the conclusion of "The Lady with the Dog" is left really and truly open: there is no suggestion, nor have we any inkling, of what the future may bring: "And it seemed that in a very little while an answer would be found, and a new and beautiful life would begin. And to both it was evident that the end was far, far away, and that the hardest, most complicated part was only just beginning."

There can be no doubt but that the policy of expounding questions without presuming to answer them—that policy which Chekhov had declared to be the writer's task—suited his style best. A full appreciation of Chekhov's work requires of the reader a certain degree of involvement, a response intellectual, or, as in the case of his love-stories, emotional, that Chekhov invites rather than commandeers. Ultimately, all depends on how Chekhov is read; but much depends on his striking the delicate balance between sentimentality and flatness.

All must surely agree that the right balance has been achieved in the final scene of "The Lady with the Dog," which is as direct an appeal to the heart as can be found in Chekhov's fiction:

> His hair was already beginning to turn grey. And it struck him as strange that he had aged so in the last few years, and lost his good looks. Her shoulders, on which he had lain his hands, were warm and shook slightly. He felt a pang of compassion for this life that was still warm and beautiful, but which would probably soon begin to fade and wither, like his own life. Why did she love him so? He had always appeared to women as something which he was not, and they had loved in him not him himself, but a creature of their own imagination, which they had sought again and again in their own lives; and then, when they perceived their mistake, they loved him all the same. And not one of them had been happy with him. Time passed, he would strike up an acquaintance, have an affair, and part, but never once had he loved; he had had everything he might wish for, only not love.
>
> And only now, when his hair had gone grey, he had fallen in love properly, genuinely—for the first time in his life.

This passage, read in the light of what we know of the author, gains a new dimension of pathos. The history of Gurov's relationships with women is a transmutation of Chekhov's history, and the essential point of the fiction was reality for him: true love had come too late, and complete happiness—poetry and communication and companionship—was impossible.

Chekhov wrote that Gurov and Anna Sergeevna "loved one another . . . as husband and wife." But how are we to explain the incongruity of this bland phrase "as husband and wife" in the context of Chekhov's entire oeuvre, in which the love of husband and wife is thwarted and cheapened—virtually never, in fact, seen to exist? Gurov and Anna are, after all, husband and wife, and he does not love his wife, nor she her husband. The irony here, whether conscious or unconscious, finds its origin in Chekhov's apparently unshakeable belief that an ideal love somewhere, somehow could exist.

—Virginia Llewellyn Smith, *Anton Chekhov and the Lady with the Dog* (London: Oxford University Press, 1973): pp. 221–22

BEVERLY HAHN ON ADULTERY IN TOLSTOY AND CHEKHOV

[In this extract, taken from her 1977 book *Chekhov: A Study of the Major Stories and Plays*, Beverly Hahn describes "The Lady with the Dog" as Chekhov's response to the challenge of Tolstoy's *Anna Karenina*.]

'The Lady with the Dog' is a tale of adultery which again seems to have the influence of Tolstoy behind it, although this time the Tolstoy of *Anna Karenina*. It is Chekhov's response to the challenge of a subject which *Anna Karenina* had made an occasion for compassion, psychological understanding and tolerance quite unlike anything we find before it in the literature of adultery; and it is, again, a testing extension of sympathies beyond even the point at which Tolstoy's sympathies end. For although Tolstoy presents Anna's predicament with unprecedented compassion, he nevertheless sees her as offending against a social and moral law, and for this there is a price to be paid. He may admire Anna, he may present her death as determined within her as an inevitable consequence of her guilt; but in fact he pursues her, determined that she shall die for what she has done: the moralist in him never quite gives rest to his instinctive sympathies. Chekhov, on the other hand, read *Anna Karenina* time and time again and knew it familiarly as 'dear *Anna*'; and the warmth of his response to Anna herself suggests that she would not have suffered the same eventual fate at his hands. His sense of the preciousness of life itself and of its unpredictability in moral terms would make it unlikely that he should feel impelled to sacrifice her for anything. So it is perhaps not surprising that his own Anna—although she is, within the much-contracted scale of 'The Lady with the Dog,' less sympathetic, less mature and altogether less splendid than Tolstoy's—is given as much satisfaction and fulfilment as the restricted terms of her situation can possibly offer. Her life as one man's wife—while she loves another—is simply that sad, bitter-sweet combination which Chekhov himself, at this stage, seems to sense and accept as the reality of things.

In all art that reflects upon the sadness of life and is burdened with the sense of its limitations, there is yet perhaps an impulse to serve life and even sometimes to celebrate its persistence and its tragically incomplete satisfactions. It is an impulse that seems to win through especially in the final phase of a great artist's work—for example, in Shakespeare, Rembrandt, Mozart and Beethoven—after earlier phases, first of exuberant discovery of sheer technical power (power exercised over a range of materials and maintaining a certain factual objectivity) and then of deepening psychological understanding and an intense confrontation of the great moral and philosophical issues of existence. That is, in the creative lives of some of our greatest artists (and Chekhov among them) we can observe three distinct phases, the third of which seems to involve a mysterious transcendence of those issues by which it has, in its second phase, been darkened and perplexed. As one would expect, it is a pattern that usually emerges from a long creative life. But there is a small group of artists whose own lives were tragically shortened and who lived in the expectation of an early death, whose apparently instinctive sensitivity to that fact seems to have caused a compression of all three phases into a span of time normally occupied by one. When Cheknov wrote 'The Lady with the Dog' he had known for some time that he was dying, and the mellowness and tolerance in the story indirectly reflect his awareness of the fact. And we find in Chekhov, as we find in Mozart, a new and quiet confidence emerging strangely but distinctly from among the tragic nuances of the art: a confidence (of which we have had some premonition in 'The Duel') that life, though often sad, can never be worthless and that it may even be self-enhancing—a confidence substantiated by the existence of the creative faculty itself. ⟨. . .⟩

'The Lady with the Dog' is not one of Cheknov's most complex stories, nor by any means his greatest. But, within the limitations of the task it sets itself, it is a moving and memorable story and one which could only have come towards the end of his career. It is, like many of his works, a testimony to his belief in the worth of human love, which, in this case, is affirmed even in the most adverse and difficult circumstances; but few of his stories manifest such mellowness and so lingering and lyrical an effect of tone. One does not wish to speak of a 'balance' in the portrayal of the joys and sorrows of Anna's and Gurov's love: rather, the story has a strange capacity—felt in the very voice of the prose—to behold the sad and bitter elements of life, to accept them for what they are, and yet to perceive even those as having a value in deepening and giving a more savoured quality to whatever is most valuable in people's lives. And it is because of this, and because of the strong sense of the pressures of time on the characters' lives, that one wants to affirm that in 'The Lady with the Dog,' Chekhov's portrayal of the mingled joy and pain of Anna's and Gurov's love is inseparable from what was, at this stage, his sense of life itself.

—Beverly Hahn, *Chekhov: A Study of the Major Stories and Plays* (Cambridge: Cambridge University Press, 1977): pp. 252–53, 263.

⚘

Vladimir Nabokov on Typical Features of Chekhov's Stories

[Vladimir Nabokov (1899–1977) was one of the twentieth century's master prose stylists. His major works include *The Gift* (1937), *The Real Life of Sebastian Knight* (1941), *Lolita* (1955), *Pnin* (1957), and *Pale Fire* (1962), and he taught literature at Wellesley, Stanford, Cornell, and Harvard. This extract is taken from his *Lectures on Russian Literature*

(1981); in it, Nabokov characterizes the main features of Chekhov tales.]

We will now repeat the different features that are typical for this and other Chekhov tales.

First: The story is told in the most natural way possible, not beside the after-dinner fireplace as with Turgenev or Maupassant but in the way one person relates to another the most important things in his life, slowly and yet without a break, in a slightly subdued voice.

Second: Exact and rich characterization is attained by a careful selection and careful distribution of minute but striking features, with perfect contempt for the sustained description, repetition, and strong emphasis of ordinary authors. In this or that description one detail is chosen to illume the whole setting.

Third: There is no special moral to be drawn and no special message to be received. Compare this to the special delivery stories of Gorki or Thomas Mann.

Fourth: The story is based on a system of waves, on the shades of this or that mood. If in Gorki's world the molecules forming it are matter, here, in Chekhov, we get a world of waves instead of particles of matter, which, incidentally, is a nearer approach to the modern scientific understanding of the universe.

Fifth: The contrast of poetry and prose stressed here and there with such insight and humor is, in the long run, a contrast only for the heroes; in reality we feel, and this is again typical of authentic genius, that for Chekhov the lofty and the base are *not* different, that the slice of watermelon and the violet sea, and the hands of the town-governor, are essential points of the "beauty plus pity" of the world.

Sixth: The story does not really end, for as long as people are alive, there is no possible and definite conclusion to their troubles or hopes or dreams.

Seventh: The storyteller seems to keep going out of his way to allude to trifles, every one of which in another type of story would mean a signpost denoting a turn in the action—for instance, the two boys at the theatre would be eavesdroppers, and rumors would spread, or the inkstand would mean a letter changing the course of the story; but just because these trifles are meaningless, they are all-important is giving the real atmosphere of this particular story.

—Vladimir Nabokov, *Lectures on Russian Literature*, Fredson Bowers, ed. (New York: Harcourt Brace and Company, 1981): pp. 262–63.

⊗

Thomas G. Winner on Lyrical Structure

[Thomas G. Winner is the author of *Oral Art and Literature of the Kazakhs of Russian Central Asia* (1958) and *Chekhov and His Prose* (1966). In this extract, taken from his essay "The Poetry of Chekhov's Prose," he discusses the tension between lyrical and prosaic elements in Chekhov's story.]

Much has been written about the lyrical tone and composition of 〈"The Lady with the Dog"〉, and the musical-poetic character of its language. It has been said that in this story the inner conflict of the chief protagonist, Gurov, is reflected by what he perceives in the reality that surrounds him; and the story has been classed 〈. . .〉 as a lyrical miniature, as a freely done sketch consisting of time fragments in which an individual penetrates into an understanding of his socio-cultural position. But most critics have described what they have called Chekhov's "lyricism" simply as a praiseworthy "device" worthy of attention. But the specificity of what creates this lyrical "tone," its formal constructs and its semiotic import, that is its relation to the multiple meanings of Chekhov's work and the significations it acquires through its relation to other artistic codes and their texts, and to the general cultural context, these questions have been ignored. 〈. . .〉

The story evolves along two parallel lines. There is its simple *fabula* which develops in time and space in a manner typical of traditional epic plot narration. Gurov meets Anna in Yalta; they have an affair; the two lovers assume their affair to be ended with their departure from Yalta. Gurov returns to Moscow, longs for Anna, follows her to the provincial town where she lives with her husband; they meet again, discover that they love each other in a new kind of love; and Anna periodically visits Gurov in Moscow. But behind the linear narration, where event follows event, another text, with other meanings, evolves. I would not call this text a subtext, the name usually applied to Chekhov's oblique texts; for it is as significant as the linear text with which it is related by a network of harmonies and oppositions. This parallel text reflects upon the conflict between two ways of living and loving: the conventional way, which permits superficial sexual affairs but keeps them in a strictly circumscribed place; and a life free from artificial falsehoods. And these two lines intertwine and intersect throughout the story, forming a complex network of harmonies and contrasts; and it is this parallelism which determines the story's lyricism, which rules over its poetic rhythms. ⟨...⟩

The so-called everyday details connecting the different sections are of particular importance, because they form a map of the psychological world of the protagonists, especially Gurov's. We can distinguish attribual details, especially those related to Gurov's vision of Anna, and other details of the surrounding world, both modelling his psychological state. Among the former, we list the following:

I. The white Pomeranian dog, Anna's blond hair, her beret, her slender, frail neck, her blushing and lowering of her glance, her beautiful grey eyes, her lorgnette, which she loses in the crowd, her perfume which envelops Gurov.

I, III, IV. Here such details become rather rare. Only two attributes of Anna are given in III, her Pomeranian dog and her lorgnette. (Since Anna does not appear in II, there are no details which describe her.) A detail of paramount importance, central to the narration and representing the same type of crisis text which is conveyed in III by the remark about the ripe sturgeon, is the poster announcing the premier of the operetta *The Geisha* which Gurov sees on alighting from the train in S. It is, later in III, against the background of this premiere, against the superficial music of the operetta played by a bad provincial orchestra, that Anna and Gurov finally complete their psychological transformation. In IV the attributes are again few: Anna's grey dress (Gurov's favorite), her pallor, serious and unsmiling expression, and her warm and trembling shoulders on which Gurov's hands rest.

Attributes of Anna serve two functions. They demonstrate both Anna's and Gurov's transformation, since they characterize her but are seen through Gurov's eyes; and they function to underscore the parallelism of the segments. Among the former are those details which show Anna's change to a more mature woman in IV (I: slender neck, blushing, lowering of eyes *vs.* IV: pallor, serious unsmiling expression, trembling shoulders). Among other details which conjoin these segments are Anna's lorgnette which binds I and III, surely a sign of her conventionality (she loses it in the crowd in I, thus in a sense metaphorically dropping her conventionality as she prepares to go to bed with Gurov). The lorgnette disappears in IV, as do other details indexical of conventionality. The second, and more important, detail, pertaining to Anna is the color grey: her "beautiful grey eyes" (*krasnye serya glaza*) in I which are transformed in IV into "his favorite grey dress" (*ego ljubimoe seroe plat'e*). The motif of greyness, taken up and supported in IV by Gurov's reflections on his greying hair, provides an important polysemic subtext. Among its many connotations is that of the ordinariness of both Anna and Gurov, of their lack of the romantic and heroic characteristic of Tolstoj's Anna and Vronskij, and of the lack of superficial glitter in contrast to the characters of *The Geisha*. Anna and Gurov are representatives of the "ordinary lives" that Chekhov depicts in so many of his works, and many other details support this connection. But the grey dress in the final segment has yet another meaning: it stands in opposition to another detail of I, namely to one of the characterizations of Yalta's elegant society where, the narrator remarks, "The older women dressed like young ones," thus stressing the superficiality and insincerity of high society in which both Gurov and Anna participate in Yalta, but from which they are divorced through the transformation achieved in IV. The grey, which becomes as indexical of Anna in IV as her white beret and her dog are in I, not only underlines the parallelism between I and IV, it unites also, as a variation, I and III. In the latter segment the color grey has a fundamentally different semantic load. It appears as the grey rug and bedcovering, and the grey dust on the inkwell in Gurov's hotel room in S., and as the grey nail-studded fence that surrounds Anna's house. Now the grey unites I and III by reversal: Anna's beautiful eyes are transformed into grey dust, dirty rugs and bedcovers and a frighteningly dissuasive fence. But the grey dust is also conjoined with the dust thrown up by the Yalta wind on the first day of the affair.

—Thomas G. Winner, "The Poetry of Chekhov's Prose: Lyrical Structures in 'The Lady with the Dog,' in *Language and Literary Theory*, Benjamin A. Stolz, I. R. Titunik, and Lubomír Doležel, eds. (Ann Arbor: University of Michigan, 1984): pp. 611, 616–17.

✦

NATHAN ROSEN ON ANNA AND GUROV

[Nathan Rosen is a professor of Russian at the University of Rochester, New York. He is also the author of *Fiction of Leonid Leonov* (1961). In this extract, Nathan Rosen studies in detail two protagonists of the story.]

The story is also one of the most personal of Chekhov's great stories. Its main character, Gurov, falls in love for the first time as he nears 40. At that same age Chekhov fell in love with the actress Olga Knipper. "The Lady with the Dog" takes place in the lovely scenery around Yalta, where Chekhov lived and where he made excursions with Olga in July 1899. The story was composed in October of that year. It is suffused with the melancholy of love in middle age, frequent partings, and intimations of mortality. Chekov was to die of consumption four years after his marriage to Olga Knipper.

The story is a marvel of economy and symmetry. The first part, three pages long, relates the first meeting of Gurov and Anna Sergeevna. The second part, five pages long, moves forward in time to portray the development of the love affair in Yalta, and closes with the departure of both Gurov and Anna. Part 3, also five pages long, is devoted to Gurov in Moscow, the awakening of his love for Anna, and his trip to visit Anna in her home town. Part 4, three pages long, focuses on a typical meeting of the two lovers in a Moscow hotel. Use of the imperfective aspect in this meeting merges the past and the future. The symmetry is clear: 3-5-5-3, with the first and the last scenes offering snapshots, as it were, of the beginning and the end, and with the action developing through time in the second and third scenes.

The title of the story—"The Lady with the Dog"—may seem puzzling since the hero of the story is not Anna Sergeevna but Gurov, whose point of view predominates. But the title also represents his point of view: when he first meets Anna, he sees her only as a blonde-haired young lady distinguished only by her small white dog. ⟨...⟩

From the very outset he is drawn to Anna Sergeevna by the one trait that separates her from his previous mistresses: her youth. She reminds him of his twelve-year old daughter. "He thought how much timidity and angularity there was still in her laugh [Anna Sergeevna's] and her manner of talking with a stranger . . . He recalled her thin, weak neck, her beautiful grey eyes." The thin weak neck indicates childlike fragility, which is reflected spiritually in her innocence, idealism, and vulnerability. She had idealistically sought a better life in marriage, but after two years (she was now 22) she despised her husband as a lackey, and did not even know what branch of the bureaucracy he worked in.

Anna Sergeevna's vulnerability takes still another form: she feels driven by forces beyond her control. Some madness drove her to Yalta; the devil and fate are (she says) responsible for her actions, and they will see to it that she will never be happy. She abdicates personal responsibility and quickly yields to Gurov—then accuses herself of shamefully giving in. Except for her idealism she has conventional values, symbolized by her lorgnette, which she loses at the pier before yielding to Gurov.

Yielding is perhaps not the right word. The scene is subtly constructed. They both stand on the pier as if waiting for someone else to come down from the steamer. Anna is silent, her eyes sparkling, and she sniffs her flowers, "not looking at Gurov." But Gurov takes no chances. He asks a perfectly ordinary question: should they not go for a ride this evening?

> She did not reply.
> Then he looked at her intently, and suddenly embraced and kissed her on the lips . . . and at once he looked round him anxiously, wondering if anyone had seen them.
> "Let us go to your place," he said softly. And they walked off together rapidly.

Anna's sexual readiness is shown in many ways, from losing her lorgnette to not looking at Gurov, but only when she fails to reply to his question does he grasp that it is time for him to act decisively and propose going to her hotel. He knows how to read signals. In Anna's case, however, those signals of her body seem to be involuntary, as if she is caught up in the whirlwind, the heat, the idleness, and her own outrage at her unfortunate marriage. ⟨. . .⟩

After Anna and Gurov have made love in her room, she cries out that she is a fallen woman whom Gurov has every right not to respect (presumably because she gave in so easily). She addresses him with the polite plural pronoun of *you* (*vy*), which is used to signal deference; this is not the pronoun that is used after sexual intimacy, and it again emphasizes her naiveté and idealism. She feels morally inferior to Gurov. Gurov, on the other hand, addresses her as *ty*, using the familiar form. (The reader should watch carefully which form of *you* is used, as a barometer of the changing relations between the lovers.) In her tears and self-castigation, says the narrator (or is it Gurov?), "she looked just like the sinner in an ancient picture"—i.e., Mary Magdalene. If this biblical association is made by Gurov, it reminds us again of his humanistic background.

Gurov finds her expression of shame utterly unexpected and out of place; none of his previous mistresses had reacted like this. He even suspects that she is putting on an act. Bored and irritated, he silently eats a piece of watermelon for half an hour while she cries. Chekhov sets up this callous reaction of Gurov's near the beginning of the story so that we can compare it, near the end of the story, with his drinking a cup of tea while she cries. ⟨. . .⟩

When Anna responds to his questions she uses the intimate *ty* form—and this is the first time she has used it. Their relationship has now become close and equal, as if their destiny is shared. Anna cannot find any comfort in Gurov's notion of living "two lives." Nor can Gurov himself. When she turns away to cry over their intolerable situation he drinks tea. This reminds us of his callous eating of a slice of watermelon in Yalta, but the context is now very different. This is not an act of indifference but, as Gerson remarks, "the expression of sadness, weariness, of bitter consciousness of the impossibility of helping his beloved." In his dejection he cannot find the strength to tell her that their meetings must sometimes come to an end—she loves and idolizes him more than ever now.

At this moment he chances to look into a mirror and sees that his hair is turning gray. He finds it strange that he has aged so much in the past few years and lost his good looks. (The two verbs rhyme in Russian: *on tak postarel, tak podurnel.*) ⟨. . .⟩

One feels like raising many questions about this paragraph. Why does Gurov suddenly discover that his hair is turning gray? If we examine the scene with care we realize that the problem is not physiological but psychological: he feels the force of life weakening within him. There are two reasons for this feeling. His Don Juan illusions about himself have faded; so have his past values—the club, the parties, the bank job, real estate. He realizes that his past life—in the light of what he has experienced at Oreanda—was completely wasted. His past values—his "public life"—are discredited. Second, he has fallen in love for the first time—in middle age; deeply involved in the life of Anna Sergeevna, he can do nothing to help her. Worse still, his love for her is the only value he still treasures—and he thinks the affair must sometime come to an end. What values would he then live by? This feeling of utter helplessness, his inability to think up any practical solution, and his terror of the future make him feel that he is old and that his life force is ebbing; and he projects his despair and his weakening life force upon Anna, so that he sees her as about to fade and wither like himself.

—Nathan Rosen, "A Reading of Chekhov's 'The Lady with the Dog,'" *Russian Language Journal* 39, nos. 132–134 (1985): pp. 13, 15–16, 22–23.

⊗

ROGER COCKRELL ON CHEKHOV'S IRONIC DETACHMENT

[Roger Cockrell is editor of *Russian Views of Pushkin* and *The Voice of a Giant: Essays on Seven Russian Prose Classics* (1985), from which this extract is taken. In it he expresses his belief that Chekhov's works attempt to combine an awareness of life's futility and hopelessness with a sense of hope. This blend reaches its fullest expression, Cockrell argues, in "The Lady with the Dog."]

The keynote here is one of ironic detachment, a view of the world which transcends any simple 'laughter through tears' formula and sets human beings and the lives they lead within an ambivalent and shifting framework of contrasting emotions and desires. It is a view which is reflected in Chekhov's art—in his short stories as well as his plays—in a subtle and complex interweaving of the tragic and the farcical, the visionary and the commonplace, the significant and the trivial.

At the very centre of Chekhov then, as both man and artist, there lies a paradoxical ambiguity which must make us wary of attaching particular labels to him. He himself reacted angrily whenever contemporary critics attempted to categorise him. As someone who once wrote, and almost certainly genuinely believed, that his works would all be forgotten within ten years after his death, he would no doubt have observed today's flourishing Chekhov industry—the spectacle of a whole host of biographers and critics trying to 'prove' now this thesis, now that—with a kind of amused despair.

'I regard trade-marks and labels as prejudicial,' he wrote in 1888. But we should remember that the nineteenth-century critic was confronted with a genuine problem when attempting to assess Chekhov. After so many writers who, from the critic's point of view at least, fell into some sort of definite category—men of the 1840s, of the 1860s, radical, liberal, conservative, populist, Slavophile, Westernist, or those such as Tolstoy or Dostoevsky who filled categories all to themselves—where was one to place Chekhov? The fact that he possessed exceptional talent as a writer served only to highlight the lack of an obvious message or unambiguous viewpoint. ⟨...⟩

Ironically, the very affair which Gurov had seen as a means of escape from the reality of his existence now forces him into an appalled realisation of its banality and futility. Just after the characteristically abortive piece of dialogue in which Gurov's attempts to convey his feelings about Anna are countered by a remark from an acquaintance to the effect that 'the sturgeon was a bit off' appear the following lines:

These words, so ordinary, for some reason suddenly infuriated Gurov and struck him as being humiliating and coarse. What primitive manners, what faces, what senseless nights, what dull and boring days! Crazy card-playing, gluttony, drunkenness, endless talk about one and the same thing. Such talk combined with totally unnecessary business activities take up the best part of your time and energy and in the end you are left with a stunted, humdrum existence: an idiotic way of life, from which there's no escape, just as though you're in prison or a lunatic asylum!

Nevertheless, despite this awareness of life's idiocy and pointlessness and this acknowledgment that there can be no lasting escape, Gurov acts decisively. He embarks on a course of action which is fundamentally different from all his previous affairs; for the first time in his life, his heart and his whole being are engaged and committed to a relationship with another person. This point alone gives the story a refreshing flavour, for the combination of committed emotion with decisive action is a rare enough occurrence in Russian literature. There is at least partly an autobiographical explanation for this course, in that Chekhov himself while writing this story was in the process of falling in love with the actress from the Moscow Arts theatre company, Olga Knipper, who was to become his wife. But there are other, more universal considerations; Chekhov seems to be saying that people who choose to lead enclosed lives, cut off from reality, are abdicating their responsibility as human beings.

Are we to infer from this that one should act at all costs, regardless of circumstances or ethical consideration? To what extent is Chekhov concerned with the moral aspects to Gurov's adulterous relationship?

In an earlier story, *On Love* (1898), the narrator, Alyokhin, faced with a similar predicament to Gurov, describes it in these terms:

I loved her dearly, profoundly but I wondered and asked myself where our love would end if we lacked the strength to fight it; it seemed improbable, but might this quiet, melancholy love of mine suddenly and rudely interrupt the happiness of her husband and children and of the entire household where I was so loved and trusted? Would this have been honest or right?

We should, however, beware of drawing too many conclusions from a passage such as this. Chekhov is neither a Dostoevsky, involving himself in tortured ethical speculations, such as whether one has the right to base one's own happiness on other people's unhappiness, nor a Tolstoy preaching a gospel of correct behaviour and condemning those who transgress the immutable moral laws—as Tolstoy does, although in the case of that other Anna, Anna Karenina, it is a very qualified condemnation. Chekhov, by contrast, is saying that there are no satisfactory answers to life's problems and that all the individual can do, once he is aware of this, is to act as best he can in the circumstances, according to his own idea of what is right and what is the truth.

If acting in this way means flying in the face of conventional morality, then so be it. For it is possible to infer from *On Love*—particularly if taken in conjunction with the two stories with which it is linked, *A Man in a Case* and *Gooseberries*—that of all man's vices there is nothing more stultifying than the propensity to surrender to routine and inertia. (We remember, too, Voinitsky's bitterly ironic observation in Act I of *Uncle Vanya* that it is considered immoral to be unfaithful to an elderly husband, but not immoral to stifle within oneself one's youth, vitality and capacity to feel.)

Although, as we see in Chapter IV of *The Lady with the Dog*, both Gurov and Anna Sergeevna are convinced that it is fate which has brought them together, Chekhov is nonetheless clearly asserting that man possesses the ability at least partly to mould his own destiny and to challenge the apparently inevitable. This is more than simply acting on one's desire, since Gurov's innermost and newly-awakened sense of values enables him to distinguish between what is true and what is false. His commitment to Anna is an expression of his true self, as opposed to the fraudulent mask he adopts for others and for everyday existence. This is made very clear in the following very Tolstoyan passage which appears in Chapter IV:

> He had two lives: one open, which everyone who was concerned saw and knew about—a life full of conventional truth and conventional falsehood, identical to the lives of his friends and acquaintances; and the other which proceeded in secret. And by some strange, perhaps coincidental combination of circumstances everything that he found important, interesting or necessary, everything in which he was sincere and did not deceive himself, everything that constituted the innermost kernel of his being took place in secret, unknown to other people; whereas everything that was false in him, the mask he adopted to hide the truth—his job at the bank, for example, the arguments at

his club, that 'inferior breed' stuff, attending anniversary parties with his wife,—all this was in the open.

Yet, despite this awakening to reality, despite Gurov's positive action and emotional commitment, nothing has been solved. On the contrary: Chekhov uses the image of two migratory birds locked up in separate cages to reflect the apparent hopelessness of the lovers' situation. Any sober assessment of Gurov and Anna's future together would give them very little chance of ever realising their happiness; they are most probably doomed to spend the rest of their lives in depressing and unhappy circumstances. He will continue living in Moscow with a wife who has become irrelevant and with people with whom he is unable to share any meaningful experiences, while she will doubtless continue to live with her lackey husband in the soulless provincial town with its grey fences and second-rate orchestra. They will probably continue to meet in just such a furtive and underhand way, in just such third-class hotels, simply because there is no realistic alternative. At one and the same time, however, they are able to see reality clearly, to recognise that life is probably meaningless and absurd and certainly fraught with difficulties and problems, and yet they are also able to maintain the vision in their hearts of at least the possibility of hope.

Chekhov's concluding words are characteristically equivocal, with the two themes forming an ironic counterpoint:

> And it seemed that it wouldn't take long for a solution to be found and then a new and wonderful life would begin; and it was clear to both of them that they were still a long, long way from the end and that the most complicated and difficult part was only just beginning.

Notice that the two halves of this concluding statement are not contrasted, but flow into each other to create one long, perfectly balanced sentence whose form reflects Chekhov's view that if man's mind must embrace reality, then equally his heart must be susceptible to dreams.

—Roger Cockrell, "Chekhov: The Lady with the Dog," in *The Voice of a Giant: Essays on Seven Russian Prose Classics*, Roger Cockrell and David Richards, eds. (Exeter, England: University of Exeter, 1985): pp. 81–83, 89–92.

Charles Stanion on the Change in Gurov

[In this essay, published in 1993, Charles Stanion discusses an indication that Gurov has changed his view of women after beginning his affair with Anna in Yalta.]

Chekhov's "The Lady with the Pet Dog" is generally regarded as a story in which a habitual lecher is transformed when he falls in love for the first time. One of the story's most impressive aspects is Dmitry Gurov's gradual metamorphosis: subtle details of action and dialogue illustrate a profound revision of his cynical attitude toward relationships with women. ⟨. . .⟩

While critics have cited ⟨. . .⟩ examples of Gurov's conversion, there is a prominent episode near the middle of the story that has gone unnoticed in this respect. In Moscow again after his affair with Anna, Gurov thinks about her continuously. While leaving a restaurant with an acquaintance, he cannot contain the impulse to mention her:

> "If you knew what a fascinating woman I met in Yalta!"
> The civil servant got into his sleigh and was about to be driven off, but suddenly turned round and called out:
> "I say!"
> "Yes?"
> "You were quite right: the sturgeon *was* a bit off."
> These words, so ordinary in themselves, for some reason hurt Gurov's feelings: they seemed to him humiliating and indecent. What savage manners!

The remark disturbs Gurov because it depreciates his veneration of Anna. He is introducing a subject of supreme personal relevance and aesthetic import, and his friend responds by free-associating from women to spoiled fish. The acquaintance not only disregards but deflates the topic of women, much to Gurov's vexation. Yet in an earlier corresponding episode Gurov himself had demonstrated the same inclination:

> there had been . . . women no longer in their first youth . . . and when Gurov had cooled to these, their beauty aroused in him nothing but repulsion, and the lace trimming on their underclothes reminded him of fish-scales.

This allusion relegates women to a category of cold-blooded, unimportant animals—like spoiled sturgeon—exactly as will the later remark by the official in the sledge. However, this attitude is no longer acceptable to Gurov. His indignant reaction to his friend's comment thus represents a 180 degree rotation in his own outlook; women and fish are no longer psychologically linked.

—Charles Stanion, "Oafish Behavior in 'The Lady with the Pet Dog,'"
Studies in Short Fiction 30, no. 3 (Summer 1993): pp. 402–3.

RICHARD FORD ON THE STORY'S EXCELLENCE

[Richard Ford, a novelist and short-story writer, is the author of the national bestseller *Independence Day*, which won the Pulitzer Prize and the PEN/Faulkner Award for Fiction in 1996. He has also received the Award for Merit in the Novel (1996), awarded by the American Academy of Arts and Letters. This extract is taken from his introduction to *The Essential Tales of Chekhov* (1998). He primarily concentrates on Chekhov's choice of characters and their unspectacular liaison.]

Back in 1964, I didn't dare to say, "I don't like this," because in truth I didn't *not* like "The Lady with the Dog." I merely didn't sense what in it was *so* to be liked. In class, much was made of its opening paragraph, containing the famously brief, complex, yet direct setting out of significant information, issues and strategies of telling which the story would eventually develop. For this reason—economy—it was deemed good. The ending was also said to be admirable *because* it wasn't very dramatic and wasn't conclusive. But beyond that, if anybody said something more specific about how the story made itself excellent I don't remember it. Although I distinctly remember thinking the story was over my head, and that Gurov and Anna were adults (read: enigmatic, impenetrable) in a way I wasn't one, and what they did and said to each other must reveal heretofore unheard of truths about love and passion, only I wasn't a good enough reader or mature enough human to recognize these truths. I'm certain that I eventually advertised actually *liking* the story, though only because I thought I should. And not long afterward I began maintaining the position that Chekhov was a story writer of near mystical—and certainly mysterious—importance, one who seemed to tell rather ordinary stories but who was really unearthing the most subtle, and for that reason, unobvious and important truth. (It is of course still a useful habit of inquiry to wonder, when the surface of reputedly great literature—and life—seem plain and equable, if something important might not be revealed upon closer notice; and also to realize that a story's ending may not always be the place to locate that something.)

In 1998, what I would say is good about "The Lady with the Dog" (and maybe you should stop here, read the story, then come back and compare notes) and indeed why I like it is primarily that it concentrates its narrative attentions *not* on the conventional hot spots—sex, deceit and what happens at the end—but rather, by its precision, pacing and decisions about what to tell, it directs our interest toward those flatter terrains of a love affair where we, being conventional souls, might overlook something important. "The Lady with the Dog" demonstrates by its scrupulous notice and detail that ordinary goings-on contain moments of significant moral choice—willed human acts judgeable as good or bad—and as such they have consequences in life which we need to pay heed to, whereas before reading the story we might've supposed they didn't. I'm referring specifically to Gurov's rather prosaic feelings of "torment" at home in Moscow, followed by his decision to visit Anna; his wife's reasonable dismissal of his suffering, the repetitiveness of trysts, the relative brevity of desire's satiation, and the necessity for self-deception to keep a small passion inflamed. These are matters the story wants us *not* to skip over, but to believe are important and that paying attention to them is good.

In a purely writerly way, I also find interest and take pleasure in Chekhov's choosing *these* characters and this seemingly unspectacular liaison upon which to stake a claim of significance and to treat with intelligence, amusement and some compassion. And superintending all these is Chekhov's surgical deployment of his probing narrator as inventor and mediator of Gurov's bland but still provocative interior life with women: "It seemed to him," the narrator says of the stolid Dmitri, "that he had been so schooled by bitter experience that he might call them [women, for course] what he liked, and yet he could not get on for two days together without 'the lower race.' In the society of men he was bored and not himself, with them he was cool and uncommunicative; but when he was in the company of women he felt free. . . ."

Finally, in "The Lady with the Dog," what seems good is Chekhov the fastidious and amused ironist who finds the right exalted language to accompany staid Gurov and pliant Anna's most unexalted amours, and in so doing discloses their love's frothy mundaneness. High on a hill overlooking Yalta and the sea, the two lovers sit and moon off, while the narrator archly muses over the landscape.

> The leaves did not stir on the trees, grasshoppers chirruped, and the monotonous hollow sound of the sea rising up from below, spoke of peace, of the eternal sleep awaiting us. So it must have sounded when there was no Yalta, no Oreanda here; so it sounds now, and it will sound as indifferently and monotonously when we are all no more. And in this constancy, in this complete indifference to the life and death of each of us, there lies hid, perhaps, a pledge of our eternal salvation, of the unceasing movement of life upon earth, of unceasing progress towards perfection.

> —Richard Ford, Introduction ("Why We Like Chekhov") to *The Essential Tales of Chekhov* (New York: Ecco Press, 1998): pp. ix–xi.

⌈℣⌉

DONALD RAYFIELD ON THE INFLUENCE OF NIETZSCHE AND SIDNEY JONES

[Donald Rayfield is a professor of Russian at Queen Mary and Westfield College, University of London, where he has taught for more than thirty years. He is the author of the monumental 1998 biography *Anton Chekhov: A Life*, and of numerous publications, including *The Cherry Orchard: Catastrophe and Comedy* (1994) and *Understanding Chekhov: A Critical Study of Chekhov's Prose and Drama* (1999), from which this extract is taken. In it, he discusses two influences on Chekhov: Nietzsche and Sidney Jones.]

All Chekhov's imagery in the last chapter—'two migratory birds . . . male and female,' the snow and the thunder, 'real life under the cover of mystery'—brings out the primitive vitality of love. The imagery of 'two migratory birds . . . forced to live in separate cages,' and a number of oriental details in the story, come from a new influence in Chekhov's work, the operetta *The Geisha* by Sidney Jones, which Chekhov mentions as the opera advertised in Anna's grey-fenced town. The idea of a wandering seducer who falls in love with a geisha, entrapped by her provincial governor, and who provides her with brief happiness before he leaves (itself a less tragic pastiche of *Madame Butterfly*) is one element from *The Geisha* which Chekhov is to use in *Three Sisters*.

The other influence is Nietzsche: Chekhov had said a year or two before that it would have been good to spend a night in a train talking to him; his aphorisms had recently been published in *New Times*; and Chekhov had earlier asked a colleague, Dr Korobov, to translate a passage of Nietzsche for *The Seagull*. In *The Cherry Orchard* Nietzsche is cited and lampooned; in 'The Lady with the Dog' Nietzsche is a serious subtext. Gurov's initial philosophy 'Lower race!' echoes Nietzsche's conviction that 'woman is created for the warrior's recreation,' that 'if you go to woman, don't forget your whip.' His reflections on a mountain-top, where everything is beautiful except what man does and thinks when he forgets 'the higher purpose of existence' is pure Nietzsche, a paraphrase of *Also sprach Zarathustra*, while the reflections on the necessary exchange of matter through death and birth likewise has a Nietzschean, anti-Christian bias. Gurov's act of commitment, of refusal to conform, his search for his lost love (so unlike the inertia of the narrator of 'The House with the Mezzanine') are proofs of a Nietzschean element in late Chekhov.

Gurov is the last of the few active heroes in Chekhov's work. The final stories and plays show a world in which the men are dying and only the women are prepared to fight on. But the message of 'The Bride' or *Three Sisters* is the natural consequence of 'The Lady with the Dog': routine is death, and turbulence—the unknown—is life. The distinction is so important that the happiness or unhappiness which the future may hold for humanity can no longer matter. For Gurov 'this little woman, in no way remarkable . . . now filled his entire life, was his misery and his joy': for Chekhov insoluble anxiety was as good an expression of the life force as was joy. The story's paragraph may start with the usual disclaimer: 'And it seemed . . . ,' but the authorial and narrative voice are united in the last main clause: 'and it was clear to both of them. . . .'

No work of Chekhov's aroused Tolstoy's ire so strongly: he felt it to be 'animal.' Subconsciously, perhaps, he detected in Chekhov's two dozen pages an explosion of the story-line and conclusion of his own *Anna Karenina*, where adultery destroys both partners and is contrasted with the affirmative course of a marriage in which sexuality has been set aside for patriarchal goals. Tolstoy seems to be vehemently denounced in Gurov's declaration—so at odds too with the Tolstoyan philosophy in 'My Life'—that we must treasure what we tell lies about. It is a vision of human happiness that thirteen years before Chekhov had decried, in a letter to his eldest brother, as 'walking about with a stolen water-melon.' Now he declares it a universal human need:

> He conjectured that everyone, under the veil of secrecy, as under the veil of night, has his real life, the most interesting one. Every individual existence is held together by a secret and, perhaps, this is partly why educated people make such intense efforts to see that personal secrets are respected.

> —Donald Rayfield, *Understanding Chekhov: A Critical Study of Chekhov's Prose and Drama* (Madison: University of Wisconsin Press, 1999): pp. 211–12

Works by
Anton Chekhov

Chekhov wrote 17 surviving plays but his main contribution to literature was in short stories. This is the most prolific area, accounting for 9 volumes of his *Collected Works* and totaling over 4,000 pages. The early period (preceding March 1888) accounts for two-thirds of Chekhov's narrative writings, including 528 published short stories, as opposed to the mere 60 short stories of his "mature" period (from March 1888 onwards).

The following list includes some of the important stories from the early period and a complete list of the 54 works published by Chekhov in his mature period (the six stories he excluded from his "Collected Works" are not listed).

"A Letter from the Landowner." (Chekhov's first traced published work) 1880.

"Running into Trouble" appears in the leading St. Petersburg comic weekly *Oskolki*. 1881.

"The Last Mohican Woman" appears in the St. Petersburg daily newspaper *Peterbugskaya gazeta*. 1882.

"Requiem" appears in the leading St. Petersburg publication *Novoye vremya*. 1883.

"The Steppe," "The Party," "An Awkward Business," "The Beauties," "The Bet," "The Seizure," "The Cobbler and the Devil." 1888.

"A Dreary Story," "The Princess." 1889.

"Thieves," "Gusev." 1890.

"Peasant Women," "The Duel." 1891.

"My Wife," "The Butterfly," "Ward Number Six," "After the Theater," "In Exile," "Neighbours," "Terror." 1892.

"An Anonymous Story," "The Two Volodyas." 1893.

"A Woman's Kingdom," "Rothschild's Fiddle," "The Black Monk," "The Student," "The Russian Master," "At a Country House," "The Head's Gardener's Story." 1894.

"Three Years," "Murder," "Ariadne," "The Order of St. Anne," "His Wife." 1895.

"The Artist's Story," "My Life." 1896.

"Peasants," "The Savage," "Home," "In the Cart." 1897.

"A Hard Case," "Gooseberries," "Concerning Love," "A Case History," "Doctor Startsev," "Angel." 1898.

"The Lady with the Dog," "New Villa," "On Official Business." 1899.

"At Christmas," "In the Hollow." 1900.

"The Bishop." 1902.

"A Marriageable Girl." 1903.

Works About
Anton Chekhov

Avilov, Lydia. *Chekhov in My Life: A Love Story*. Translated by David Magarshak. London: J. Lehman, 1950.

Bitsilli, Peter. *Chechov's Art: A Stylistic Analysis*. Translated by Toby Clyman and Edwina Jannie Cruise. Ann Arbor, Michigan: Ardis Publishers, 1983.

Bruford, W. H. *Chekhov and His Russia*. New York: Oxford University Press, 1948.

Chudakov, A. P., *Chekhov's Poetics*. Translated by Edwina Jannie Cruise and Donald Dragt. Ann Arbor, Mich.: Ardis, 1983.

Clayton, J. Douglas, ed. *Chekhov Then and Now: The Reception of Chekhov in World Culture*. New York: Peter Lang, 1997.

Clyman, Toby W., ed. *A Chekhov Companion*. Westport, Conn.: Greenwood Press, 1985.

Debreczeny, Paul, and Thomas Eekman, eds. *Chekhov's Art of Writing: A Collection of Critical Essays*. Columbus, Ohio: Slavica, 1977.

Eekman, T. ed., *Anton Chechov, 1860–1960: Some Essays*. Leiden: E. J. Brill, 1960.

Ehrenburg, Ilya. *Chekhov, Stendhal and Other Essays*. London: Macgibbon and Kee, 1962.

Gerhardi, William. *Anton Chekhov: A Critical Study*. London: Macdonald and Co., 1949.

Gorky, Maxim. *Reminiscences of Tolstoy, Chekhov and Andreev*. Translated by Katherine Mansfield, S. S. Koteliansky, and Leonard Woolf. London: The Hogarth Press, 1948.

Hingley, Ronald. *Russian Writers and Society 1825–1904*. New York: McGraw-Hill Book Company 1967.

———. *Chekhov: A Biographical and Critical Study*. London: George Allen and Unwin, 1966.

Jackson, Robert Louis, ed. *Reading Chekhov's Text*. Evanston, Ill.: Northwestern University Press, 1993.

———. *Chekhov: A Collection of Critical Essays.* Englewood Cliffs, N.J.: Prentice Hall, 1967.

Johnson, Ronald L. *Anton Chekhov: A Study of Short Fiction.* New York: Twayne, 1993.

Karlinsky, Simon, ed. *Anton Chekhov's Life and Thought: Selected Letters and Commentary.* Translated by Henry Heim and Simon Karlinsky. Berkeley: University of California Press, 1973.

Kirk, Irina. *Anton Chekhov.* Boston: Twayne Publishers, 1981.

Kramer, K. D. *The Chameleon and the Dream.* Paris: Mouton, 1970.

Lafitte, Sophie. *Tchekhov 1860–1904.* Paris: Librarie Hatchette, 1971.

Le Fleming, L. S. K. "The Structural Role of Language in Chekhov's Later Stories," *The Slavonic and East European Review* 48 (1970): 323–40.

Llewellyn Smith, Virginia, *Chekhov and the Lady with the Dog.* London: Oxford University Press, 1973.

Magarshack, David. *Chekhov: A Life.* New York: Grove Press, 1955.

Meister, Charles W. *Chekhov Criticism: 1880 through 1986.* Jefferson, N.C.: McFarland, 1989.

Melchinger, Siegfried. *Anton Chekhov.* New York: Frederick Ungar Publishing 1972.

Popkin, Cathy. "Chekhov's Corpus: Bodies of Knowledge," *Essays in Poetics* 18 (1993): 44–72.

Pritchett, V. S. *Chekhov: A Spirit Set Free.* London: Hodder and Stoughton, 1988.

Rayfield, Donald. *Chekhov: The Evolution of His Art.* New York: Barnes and Noble, 1975.

Simmons, Ernest J. *Chekhov: A Biography.* Boston: Little, Brown and Company, 1962.

Stowell, Peter. *Literary Impressionism, James and Chekhov.* Athens: University of Georgia Press, 1980.

Toumanova, Princess Nina Andronikova. *Anton Checkhov: The Voice of Twilight Russia.* New York: Columbia University Press, 1937.

Tulloch, John. Chekhov: *A Structuralist Study.* New York: Harper and Row, 1980.

Wellek, Rene, and Nonna D. Wellek, eds. *Chekhov: New Perspectives.* Englewood Cliffs, N.J.: Prentice Hall, 1984.

Winner, Thomas. *Chekhov and His Prose.* New York: Holt, Rinehart and Winston, 1966.

Index of
Themes and Ideas

function of character in, 49–50; critical views on, 41–53; cyclical shape of, 41–43; and Easter, 53; language in, 42–43; Lukerya and Vasilisa as heroes in, 51–53; Lukerya in, 38, 40, 48, 49–51; nature in, 38, 41, 42; and optimism, 38–39; plot summary of, 38–39; point of view in, 47–49; river in, 42; suffering giving meaning to life in, 41–43; Vasilisa in, 38, 39, 40, 42, 43, 44, 45, 48, 49, 50–52; Ivan Velikopolsky in, 38, 39, 40, 41, 42, 43, 44–45, 46–47, 48–49, 52–53